# The Magic Of Easter

To Nikita
With Very Best
Wishes

A E Reynolds

poetry *pt* today

# THE MAGIC OF EASTER

Edited by
Suzy Walton

First published in Great Britain in 2001 by Poetry
Today, an imprint of
Penhaligon Page Ltd, Remus House, Coltsfoot Drive,
Peterborough. PE2 9JX

© Copyright Contributors 2001

All rights reserved. No part of this publication may be
reproduced, stored in a retrieval system, or transmitted
in any form or by any means, without prior permission
from the author(s).

A Catalogue record for this book is available from the
British Library

ISBN 1 86226 692 1


Typesetting and layout, Penhaligon Page Ltd, England
Printed and bound by Forward Press Ltd, England

# *Foreword*

*The Magic Of Easter* is a compilation of poetry, featuring some of our finest poets. This book gives an insight into the essence of modern living and deals with the reality of life today. We think we have created an anthology with a universal appeal.

There are many technical aspects to the writing of poetry and *The Magic Of Easter* contains free verse and examples of more structured work from a wealth of talented poets.

Poetry is a coat of many colours. Today's poets write in a limitless array of styles: traditional rhyming poetry is as alive and kicking today as modern free verse. Language ranges from easily accessible to intricate and elusive.

Poems have a lot to offer in our fast – paced 'instant' world. Reading poems gives us an opportunity to sit back and explore ourselves and the world around us.

# Contents

|  |  |  |
|---|---|---|
| Easter Gift | Floriana Hall | 1 |
| Easter Sunday | Fae D Wason | 2 |
| The Meaning Of Life | Erika Rollinson | 3 |
| Easter, When I Was A Child | E M Taylor | 4 |
| Easter Promise | Finnan Boyle | 5 |
| An Easter Egg | Emmalene Maguire | 6 |
| Snow White | James Lucas | 7 |
| Easter Time | Paul Anthony | 8 |
| Easter | John M Davis | 9 |
| Easter | Paul Douglas | 10 |
| Untitled | Caroline Halliday | 11 |
| Easter | Betty Green | 12 |
| Oh, My Saviour | Terry Wray | 13 |
| The Meaning Of Easter | Sarah Bell | 14 |
| Calvary | John Joinson | 15 |
| Reminded | John Ellerton | 16 |
| Easter | Hazell Dennison | 17 |
| Easter Glory! | Margaret McHugh | 18 |
| Easter Sunday | Veronica Quainton | 19 |
| Easter Thoughts | Clifford Rudall | 20 |
| My Easter Garden | Viv-Lionel Borer | 22 |
| Simon | Jackie Lapidge | 24 |
| Easter | Barbara Davies | 26 |
| Calvary | Doreen Sowden | 27 |
| Easter | Dianne Core | 28 |
| Easter.The Message | John Morrison | 29 |
| Easter's Hearts Of Stone | Des O'Donnell | 30 |
| Easter | Frances Cox | 31 |
| Easter | Mike Bullock | 32 |
| I Peter | Amelia Wilson | 33 |
| His Life For Mine | Mary Neill | 34 |
| At Eastertime | John Harrold | 35 |
| Calvary In Penarth | Nigel Latham | 36 |
| Faith Today | T W Denis Constance | 37 |
| Easter Courage | Albert Boddison | 38 |

| | | |
|---|---|---|
| The Family Of Man | A E Reynolds | 39 |
| Spring Has Sprung! | Cheryl Mann | 40 |
| Resurrection | Karlena Jambor | 41 |
| Untitled | Jack Clancy | 42 |
| From Death To Life | Marion Staddon | 43 |
| Easter | Ivy Squires | 44 |
| Easter Communion | Daphne Foreman | 45 |
| Easter | Daphne Robinson | 46 |
| Easter | Tina Rooney | 47 |
| Easter | Owen Edwards | 48 |
| An Easter Egg Invasion | Karl Jakobsen | 49 |
| Easter | N Reeves | 50 |
| Spirit Poem For Easter | Olga Johnson | 51 |
| Spring Has Sprung! | Chrissie McGrew | 52 |
| Easter | J R Dixon | 53 |
| Easter | Jean Smithers | 54 |
| Good Friday | Ernie Cummings | 55 |
| We Do Not Listen | Michael Alan Fenton | 56 |
| Dominus Crucifixus | M Keeling-Roberts | 57 |
| Easter Sorrow, Easter Joy | John Cook | 59 |
| Easter | Doreen Hanley | 60 |
| Worship | Beryl Johnson | 61 |
| Eastertime | Joan Miles | 62 |
| The Death Of The Son | David John Dunbar | 63 |
| Easter Glory | Angus W MacDonald | 64 |
| Easter | Dannika Webber | 65 |
| The World Seems Now Too Crowded | J S Games | 66 |
| Easter Fun | M Griffiths | 67 |
| Lenten Blooming; Easter Glory | John A Mills | 68 |
| Whoa! Darryl | Harry Swanger | 69 |
| Easter | Robert Henry Lonsdale | 70 |
| Judy Or Jesus It's Easter Again | Doug Smith | 71 |
| Easter Day | Andrew A Duncan | 72 |
| Easter Memories | Zoe French | 73 |
| Easter's Almost Here | Margaret Whitton | 74 |
| Easter Herald | Andrew Bray | 75 |
| Easter | M Wise | 76 |

| | | |
|---|---|---|
| Good Friday | Joyce Piper | 77 |
| Easter | Kim Davenport | 78 |
| Easter | J R Hirst | 79 |
| No Doubt | Jean Thornton | 80 |
| Easter | John Paulley | 81 |
| Christ's Donkey | Ted Harriott | 82 |
| Easter Thoughts | Ruth Shallard | 83 |
| Easter | Judith Herrington | 84 |
| The Samaritan Had The Essence | Allan Bula | 85 |
| Memory Of Easter | Norma Griffiths | 86 |
| The Long Journey (Friday, 14th April 2000) | Joyce Metcalfe | 87 |
| A Special Time | Gloria Hargreaves | 88 |
| Eastertime | M Campbell | 89 |
| When Easter Approaches | Jeanette Gaffney | 90 |
| Rose And Apple | Beatrice Gwynn | 91 |
| You Devil You | Susan Olwen Papworth | 93 |
| Egg-stacy | Peter Miles | 94 |
| Angel Watching | David E Nettles | 95 |
| Easter | Thomas Usher | 96 |
| Cancelled Debt | Kathy Rawstron | 97 |
| Easter! | Cassy Dmore | 98 |
| An Easter Service | Phillip Stringer | 99 |
| The Reality Of Easter | Natalie Jagger | 100 |
| Easter | Samantha Vaughan | 101 |
| I Wish That I Had Been There | Phillippa Benson | 102 |
| Easter | Dolly Little | 103 |
| Special Thoughts Of Easter | Octavia Hornby | 104 |
| Easter | Daniela Lampariello Taylor | 105 |
| An Easter Verse | E R Bridgewater | 106 |
| The Precious Son | Joan Smith | 107 |
| Commercialism | Sheila Graham | 109 |
| Hosanna | E Griffin | 110 |
| The Magic Of Easter | Audrey Randall | 111 |
| Eastertime | Michelle Knight | 112 |
| Easter Bells | Gloria Joice | 113 |
| Easter | Emily Hanney | 114 |
| Easter Is:- | Betty Nevell | 115 |

| | | |
|---|---|---|
| Easter | Kathleen Glover | 116 |
| Easter Echoes | K E Warne | 117 |
| What Easter Really Means | Yvonne Charles | 118 |
| Easter | Malcolm Goat | 119 |
| The Judgement | Marion Gray | 120 |
| The Second Coming | Carole Wale | 121 |
| Continuity | Malcolm Peter Mansfield | 122 |
| Easter | Elsie Karbacz | 123 |
| Easter Faith | Sarah Bridges | 124 |
| Easter | Lucy Adams | 125 |
| Easter Blessing | Patricia Maloney | 126 |
| Easter | Sylvia Berwick | 127 |
| Eastertime | Marie Knowles | 128 |
| Easter Matters! | Rosalind Weaver | 129 |
| Easter Day | Linda M Adams | 130 |
| Easter | Kathleen Collins | 131 |
| Easter Mass | John Paget | 132 |
| Easter | Angus Richmond | 133 |
| The Beauty Of Easter | Jean P Edwards McGovern | 134 |
| Eggs | Harold Wonham | 135 |
| Easter | Nan Downs | 136 |
| Rebirth | Neata Todd | 137 |
| Eastertime | Doris Lilian Critchley | 138 |
| Teuton Queen | Andrew Perrins | 139 |
| A Paschal Sun | Francis McDermott | 140 |
| Easter | K Baird | 141 |
| Remember This | Mary Lawson | 142 |
| Simon's Story | Jennie Metcalfe | 143 |
| Easter Message | Kathleen Potter | 145 |
| Easter | Valerie Gaynor | 146 |
| Easter | Jason Donald | 147 |
| Easter | Abbie Latham | 148 |
| The Blessing Of Eastertide | Blanche Rice | 149 |
| Sing For Easter | Jalil Kasto | 150 |
| Eastertide | Monica Redhead | 151 |
| Silence This Easter | M Wood | 152 |
| Easter Hope | O Miller | 153 |
| Easter Deer | Joanna Dicks | 154 |

*Easter Gift*

Our God, our Saviour, our hope, our redemption,
His human form from pain no exemption,
   Suffered and died for our sins
      So our new life of grace could begin.

Wooden cross, insults tossed, humanity's loss,
   Sepulchre space,
      Tombstone in place
         Where is His beautiful face?

Betrayed, dismayed, the women stayed and prayed,
Moaned and groaned, what price He paid -
   Rolling stone,
      Stepping stone
         Bestowed on Easter morn.

Resurrection, new direction for our imperfection,
   Brilliant light,
      Clothed in white, glorious sight.
The beginning, not the end
      Bestowed on Easter morn.

*Floriana Hall*

## *Easter Sunday*

Forty days were spent in mourning,
Now the hour's arrived
To celebrate this happy morning
Now He's once more alive.
Lilies and vestments are festival white.
Candles flicker and show
The silver vessels high and bright
And the incense wafting low.
We rejoice and keep this holy day,
And thank our living Lord
For laying down His life that way
Then giving us His word
That as was said in His days before
We'd live forever more.

*Fae D Watson*

## *The Meaning Of Life*

As I knelt beside my Mother's bed
with her hand upon my head,
she said to me, 'My child
Life is but a dream.'

All the worries and fears,
Which troubled one's younger years
Just simply disappear.
Instead come the memories,
of husband and family
all linked in harmony.

In the autumn glow,
one begins to understand,
what one really wants to know.
What life is all about,
Its motive and purpose,
to love one another and,
eventually surface in God's heaven above.
Where there is only love, that is life's purpose.

*Erika Rollinson*

## *Easter, When I Was A Child*

The month of April, a milestone each year
As a child it is a day of joy, with no fear
On the twenty-fourth a special day, my birthday
Closely by comes a Sunday, Easter Day
Chocolate eggs for both, when I was a child

Colourful boxes, each one a bright square
Hollow eggs, a chocolate shell alone so bare
Or an egg, with a china mug to keep
Drink nightly cocoa, before you count the sheep
Chocolate eggs for Easter, when I was a child

Inside this one, I find some chocolate sweets
Now that is what I call a special treat
To eat them now, or shall I save for later
Then maybe I could share, they number eight
Chocolate eggs till Christmas, when I was a child

Look at the shelves today, eggs with chocolate bars
Even those, that look like they come from Mars
All the favourites, tempting mothers to buy
Which will it be, grandparents are on a high
Easter eggs with extras, I wish I was a child . . . again

*E M Taylor*

## *Easter Promise*

On Calvary's hill one fateful day
An event forced mankind to pray
For the Son of God
Who had taken the mantle of Abraham's rod
Was crucified to death
As his mother stood with bated breath
The Apostles cried
The eyes of the blind opened wide
As his charismatic life ebbed away
On this dark lightning-charged day
The crowd taunted and bated
Mankind waited
For the prophesied resurrection
Casting away the shackles of evil's insurrection

*Finnan Boyle*

## *An Easter Egg*

I hand you the egg, you look up and grin,
Eager to open the box and begin,
You jump off my lap, and beg for a game,
Running and chasing and calling my name.

Sometimes I am sad,
                When I look at you
At the life you have known,
                    And what you've been through
But I know that you trust me,
                To stay by your side
And the honour of you,
                Fills me with pride.

I hope when you're old you won't dwell in your head,
On anything but the
              joy
                    of that big Easter egg.

*Emmalene Maguire*

## Snow White

The direct bludgeoning tracks of vehicles,
that playful interweave of tiny cycle movements,
re-asserting the danger of one to the other;
enigma, police tracking the sole delinquent?
The delightful, yet temporary, sweet white blossom
on each and every hedge and bush,
the roofs of houses, winter tell-tale of inner warmth
cars, out all night on the driveways,
reminiscing though opposing, Henry 'Fords' dictum
'Choose whatever colour you like
providing it is always snow-white.'
Where a stationary car has moved on
an exact, impenetrable but menacing black hole;
against the snow brilliance, road markings
white lines now dulled to ochre-grey;
the sky, cobalt, sun's diversion with floating snow-clouds,
the sudden urge, to retain this passing total image, -
'Where did I put the camera?'
So, soon, the magic melts, we glory again, nature's natural.

*James Lucas*

## *Easter Time*

Easter bunny so full of life
Chocolate egg bought for my wife
Day of fun and frolic too
On this day what will you do?

Children fill themselves with sweets
Parents take them out for treats
Laugh and play throughout the day
'How disgusting' some will say.

Day at the beach for some no doubt
Kids on nerves will get a clout
Funfair rides and day trips too
Some will go off to the zoo.

Shops and café open for all
For your custom they will call
People rest, lots will play
On this a special Easter day.

Day will end with wine and food
Fun was had, a happy mood
Sleep will come at end of day
'Thank you Lord,' I hear some say.

*Paul Anthony*

*Easter*

Easter!
Feast or
Festival vernal,
Timeless, eternal;
Resurrection
From rejection -
Festival
Pre aestival
Of the High Priest or
Saviour of Easter.

*John M Davis*

## *Easter*

*Easter* tells us Jesus died and that He rose again.
*Easter* tells us Jesus suffered agonising pain.

It didn't have to be that way, He could have changed the plan;
but Jesus knew it must be so, for He was now a man.

A man who was the Son of God with powers absolute,
yet could not choose to free Himself from agonies acute.

For He had come to save mankind and not Himself from sin
and as the last breath left Him, a New Age entered in.

An Age when man must now repent for what had gone before,
that he might be forgiven and have New Life evermore.

An Age when man toward God must turn and love Him
and his neighbour,
whom he must treat an equal if he would know his Saviour.

*Easter* tells us Jesus lives, even though He died.
*Easter* tells us Jesus walks, beside us, stride for stride.

It doesn't have to be that way, yes, you can change things too,
for God has given you a choice, it's simply up to you.

To walk with God and Jesus will bring eternal Peace,
and while you live upon this Earth, your life extends its lease.

You may be young, you may be old, or somewhere in between,
but age has little bearing, when you've seen what can't be seen!

*Paul Douglas*

## *Untitled*

For me Easter is a time of new beginnings
my time to give gifts and love
to remember what we have
God gave his son Jesus
I give love and guidance
eggs, the symbol of rebirth
my realisation, of love

*Caroline Halliday*

*Easter*

Easter to me brings much hope,
With memories that make life far easier to cope.
One sees new life come to flower and tree,
And each new day brings a different vision to see.
The days can be a little longer,
And you give thanks as you begin to feel much stronger.
You feel you could do with more and more fresh air,
Never give in or it could lead to despair.
Although I love the different seasons,
Easter to me brings with it many reasons,
To herald each new day with joy,
And all kinds of tactics employ.

*Betty Green*

## *Oh, My Saviour*

Now as I gaze upon the cross
I see my Saviour hanging there,
Thorns bedeck his brow as a crown,
Nails his hands and feet have pierced.
There he hangs between two thieves.
Oh, my Saviour, oh my Lord.

You don't deserve this punishment
For all you did, was only good.
Oh, how short their memory is.
You were gentle, meek and mild
Yet they hung you on the cross
Oh, my Saviour, oh my Lord.

Now as I gaze upon the cross
A sense of guilt comes over me,
I realise my present sins
Are crucifying him again.
'Lord, forgive me, oh, I plead.'
Oh, my Saviour, oh my Lord.

*Terry Wray*

## *The Meaning Of Easter*

What's the meaning of Easter?
I asked the children today.
'It means chocolate eggs and goodies
and time off school to play!'

But it was the real reason
I wanted them to know
How Jesus gave his life for us
so many years ago

They thought for just a moment
and scratched their little heads
'If Jesus died at Easter . . .
Who'd eat his Easter eggs?'

    *Sarah Bell*

## *Calvary*

Three crosses upon a hill set high
With three men nailed on them to die
Two criminals sentenced by the court
Our Lord there false charges brought
One thief mocked Jesus and hurled abuse
The other thief didn't offer any excuse
'Today you'll be with me in paradise' He said
The Holy One with crown of thorns on His head
They offered Him wine or vinegar to drink
Jesus refused He wanted a clear head to think
'Father forgive them they know not what they do'
The Roman soldiers and the gathered few
Three long hours Jesus suffered on the cross
No one had realised the world's great loss
'It is finished' Jesus agonisingly cried
In the moment He gave up the ghost and died

*John Joinson*

## Reminded

Bedsores pitted skin, scars looked like the whip.
Jesus suffered agonising lashes,
condemned, crucified after his gown ripped.
Bedsores pitted skin, scars looked like the whip.
A surgeon's team then nurses checked the drip.
Endless stream, friends and family gnashes.
Jesus suffered an agonising trip.
Jesus suffered agonising lashes.

*John Ellerton*

*Easter*

Blossom hangs heavily scenting the fresh spring air.
Rabbits playing gleefully, lambs gambol without a care.
Easter is here with fluffy yellow chicks and Easter eggs galore.
Children parading their Easter bonnets, some sit watching on the floor,
Daffodils swaying in the gentle breeze bright like the golden sun,
Everyone is happy sharing in the Easter fun.
But take time out to reflect the true meaning of it all.
Go to church, say your prayers give thanks when the church bells call,
Be kind to others, live rewarding lives and let's all rejoice.
This is the resurrection of our dear Lord Jesus Christ.

*Hazell Dennison*

## *Easter Glory!*

Oh, blessed Easter
The time of sorrow and joy
Sorrow for the way Christ died
Upon a cross at Easter-tide
Good Friday we cannot forget
That sorrowful day still lingers yet
The pain and suffering that He bore
We will remember for ever more
But now He is in heaven above
Leaving us His boundless love
To help us all along life's way
So say a little prayer each day
There is another side to Easter
So glorious and bright
The golden sun now shining bright
Instead of winter's cold, dark night
Warming us with its golden glow
We forget the rain, the frost and snow
Here is spring, all new and bright
The budding trees, the flowers in bloom
Filling every inch of room
That they have found
To dance and sway
On the soft green ground
Shedding their scent and fragrance everywhere
Especially, in a bluebell wood
Where masses of bluebells can be found
Turning the forest into a sea of blue
Amidst the green and fertile ground
And an angel looks down from above
To see for himself
That all is good

*Margaret McHugh*

## *Easter Sunday*

The light breaks through revealing the dawn
On this glorious, blessed Easter morn
It is our Lord's resurrection day
Victory over sin is ours to stay
The climax of his life on earth
He broke the bonds and gave us new birth
Alleluia! Our Jesus is risen
And opened for us the gates of heaven
Come let us give thanks and heartfelt praise
On this most holy of holiest days
With hearts raised high we bend the knee
To our Saviour and King who has set us free
All glory and honour to thee we sing
The love of our hearts dear Jesus we bring
The church bells ring in joyful accord
Giving praise and glory to our living Lord.

*Veronica Quainton*

## *Easter Thoughts*

O Muse, lend me your aid,
For 'tis Easter, and a poem would be made.
Its story, mankind seems to have mislaid.
Renew its message and thus to the world give
Central aid, in remembering what God has done for man
Through the centuries; our recall can now span
With literate aid, historical events that testify
To God's wondrous sacrifice when Himself He gave,
In order mankind to save from eternal demand,
Wherein the mighty laws, which govern us, and our future to behold,
To redeem us with salvation from damnation to unfold.

O wondrous Angels, no secret to thee,
How God let Himself be sacrificed on that
Golgothic Hill of Calvary.
To our feeble thought, our vision dim,
Hidden with purpose, only Love can reveal,
A destiny that does not depend on a passing whim,
But can seek out, with desires and questions unanswered
until the last time,
When resurrection with Him will be our event,
From dreams to reality, a mighty step
Our future lives to reveal.

Let not this prose be a satisfaction that words can use,
In lieu of visions embrace, with events to peruse
With Meta eye.
No boundered rhyme, but Truth to seek
Through thoughts lent to the meek,
Yet mighty as the wonderful sky
That shelters man, a cover so high.

Renew our thoughts with feelings true,
A guide to show the way;
Reveal to us, as *Jesus*, the path anew;
We must restart our journey if by the way
We falter and wander from the path - to stray
Amid fields that allure with scents so sweet,
Tantalising our thoughts with dreams, that do not meet
The longing for return to *God's Bright Day.*

*Clifford Rudall*

## My Easter Garden

Under and around the weeping willow tree,
When gardens bloom and songbirds sing,
The first flowers of the spring morning that I see,
The scented air of fragrant flowers.

With their small, well-formed trumpets raised so bold,
The lively lambs, the longer hours,
Their creamy heads in contrast to the daffodils gold.
With warmer days and nights so clear,
As the spring winds make them sway.
I stroll through lands my head held high,
Just like pretty ballerinas in a theatrical display.

And watch the beautiful clouds roll by,
The breeze is thy choreographer thus making your beauty around
                                                          at this time,
I pick some flowers here and there, the sun shining,
A carpet of cream coloured dancers all along the ground,
At this Easter time.

Nature's gifts so pure and free; so many eggs,
To enjoy this wonderful time, to eat plenty,
Like rays of sunlight through their fingers, their faces covered
                                                          in chocolate,
The time has come for the song to begin; How many eggs I had today.

Things would not seem so desolate and bleak,
If only in the near future could I take a peek.
Night is nigh, and birds who sing and play,
Children eat their eggs and rest.
Settle in their nests and beds, until another day,
All is quiet yet suddenly comes a sound,
The birds want their worms and children want their eggs now!

With hands outstretched their mouths opened,
Watching all around with their glaring eyes.
Swooping across the room with speed,
For their kills with a hungry greed.

My eyes and heart are so heavy, I make a sigh,
My heart and eyes begin to feel pain,
A strange feeling yet again.

*Viv-Lionel Borer*

## Simon

I was just passing through.
Just a few days there looking for work.
I can turn my hand at most things -
A bit of carpentry, sheep herding, labouring.
I'm pretty strong.
I suppose that's why they picked on me.
'Here!' the rough soldier yelled.
'You carry it!'
Well, you don't argue, do you?
Not with them.
And the man did look done in -
Pale, exhausted. Seems he'd had a beating too.
Anyway, he fell, and couldn't lift it anymore.
Well, that's the way it is.
I felt sorry for him, just the same.
He didn't really look the criminal -
More of a dreamer, I'd have thought.
So I lifted it up and carried it to the top of the hill.
Then they pushed me out of the way -
Not so much as a 'thank you'.
I stayed and watched.
People were wailing, cursing, babbling.
I didn't understand much.
The man was very calm, I thought,
Considering the death he had to face.
He said a few words,
Hanging there.
But I didn't understand.
About three it got very dark -
Strange, it was,
Almost pitch black in mid-afternoon.
Then the man cried out.
A terrible cry.
And then he died.

The people went away - except a few
Who stayed behind
To take the body down.
Peaceful he looked.
I don't know what became of him after that.
But sometimes I can see that calm, pale face.
It seems to be printed somewhere on my mind.
Strange, it should haunt me all these years.
I was just passing through.

   *Jackie Lapidge*

## *Easter*

Easter:  Means much to a Christian mind
To give thanks to the One who saved mankind
A crucified Christ nailed to a tree
So that mortals on earth from sin shall be free
He came here to dwell poor sinners to save
By the power of God to rise from the grave
Glory and praise to our Saviour above
Who grants us forgiveness, unconditional love
Lord walk at our side and live in our heart
In our daily tasks please - to play a big part
Give us your blessings, for this God we pray
Humbly to serve You with love every day
We sing out your praises, our Saviour divine
As we kneel at the Cross on this Easter time.

*Barbara Davies*

## *Calvary*

Grim place of pain, a darkened sky, a lonely cross upon a hill,
Where my dear Lord was caused to die, the image haunts the
                                                  memory still
Recalls a man born just like me; but kind and gentle, wise and strong.
Who healed the sick, the hungry, fed, taught peace and love,
                                                  and righted wrong.
A man . . . but more than man is this, this Son of God, this Lord of all.
Betrayal by a traitor's kiss, made hearts to break and tears to fall.
But death could not a Saviour hold, the grave could not His prison be.
The Lamb is in His Father's fold. An empty cross on Calvary.
Where once were thorns upon His brow, our Lord is crowned
                                                        with glory now.

*Doreen Sowden*

## *Easter*

A mother stands at the foot of a cross
Waiting and weeping.
A son nailed to the cross is suffering
His mother absorbs the pain, silent tears
Coursing down her cheeks.
With one last cry he leaves the world
Leaving love and emptiness
Imprinted on his mother's heart.
And a timeless legacy of *unconditional*
Love to the world.

*Dianne Core*

## *Easter. The Message*

A gentle man a good man
Endowed with God's love and power
Weep not for this man
Curse not this travesty
He was the centrepiece
In God's rich tapestry

*John Morrison*

## *Easter's Hearts Of Stone*

Sleep easy he said
Jesus is dead
And finally entombed
Within the womb of Mother Earth
Who never yet had given birth -
And yet . . . the High Priest wondered

There was no place here for seeds of doubt
So guards were set
To keep Him in . . . and others out
Who'd Corpus Christi steal away
And in the brand new dawn of day
Proclaim He is . . . Arisen!

Awakened aware, alarmed . . . a shout!
The High Priest paled
God's Son was out:
They reported in what had to be said -
Oh why *couldn't* He . . . have stayed in His bed?
The stone . . . the stone was rolled away

His own? . . . just blanked it -
Magdalene was mad - deranged,
And yet they found it very strange
That the heavy stone . . . was rolled away -
Though doubting Thomas spoke for most
Demanding proof of this . . . Holy Ghost!

In an age of reason where Science rules
Are we simply taken in . . . as fools?
So by what acid test can Faith be proved?
Credo . . . by Love we all are moved
Please don't abort your Hope today
Ask Our Father to roll your stone away.

*Des O'Donnell*

*Easter*

Christmas celebrations past
Followed by the Lenten fast
Nature's preparations seen
As burgeoning buds of springtime green
Appear on boughs, in woodland glade
As winter snows begin to fade.
The April sun, its fitful glow
To finite man divine gifts show
That mortal death is not the end
Because, to earth Christ did descend
For that at-one-ment with frail man
His sacrifice - our sins to ban
On Calvary upon that cross
(His mother Mary's saddest loss).
But, three days later Christ arose
Of death's dark sting he did dispose
For, one day, from our earthy tomb
Our souls like springtime flowers will bloom
As Easter Day restores to earth
God's glorious gifts which from our birth
Surround us all - each year restored
Through risen Christ - our Saviour Lord.

*Frances Cox*

*Easter*

Strung out on a cross
So pale and helpless
Looking at a world
Of pride and hate
Gave Himself for us
Without a flicker
So that we could have
A different fate.

How can we reject
What You've done for us
Putting out of mind
Your sacrifice
Going our own way
While You stand crying
See the tears a-flowing
From Your eyes.

Help us to renounce
Our thoughtless striving
Give it all to You
Who wants to know
Every little thing
We gladly hand You
Just like sheep, to follow
Where You go.

    *Mike Bullock*

## *I Peter*

I denied Him! Did you know? I denied Him,
After all my big brave words, I let Him down
I even said that I would die beside Him.
But you have to bear a cross, to win a crown.

As I stood before the fire, they asked the question,
And I swore that I had never known the man,
Never knew this Jesus! God forgive me,
And then like all the rest, I turned and ran.

I failed Him in his darkest hour of torment.
They nailed Him to a cross, I guess you knew.
If He had been your friend, would you have left Him?
Or has it happened just the same to you?

But the wonder of it all is, He forgave me,
He rose again, and sent a word for me.
The women, from the tomb, brought us a message,
That we would see Him there in Galilee.

And so we did, our blessed Lord and Master.
The nail prints in His hands, and wounded brow.
He came to comfort us, though we forsook Him.
I never could deny my Saviour, now.

*Amelia Wilson*

## *His Life For Mine*

The coming of April with its brightness of flower,
The rain is more gentle with more daylight hour,
The buds on the trees just beginning to show
Also it is less likely to snow.
The children talk of Easter eggs
And how many they will get,
But most of all it is the time for Christ
We should never never forget,
For without his coming where would we be.
It is a time for reflection
On his saving grace,
His forgiveness he gave us
With unconditional love.
He lay down his life for the love of the world,
This sacrifice was the greatest of all.
Although we moan about life's daily strife,
Till the end of may days
I will thank Christ
*For my life.*

*Mary Neill*

## *At Eastertime*

At Eastertime
Jesus died,
women cried,
men jeered,
others cheered,
at Eastertime.

At Eastertime,
Jesus buried,
others hurried,
home and away
for another day,
at Eastertime.

At Eastertime,
Jesus ascended
from descended,
no more pain
alive again,
at Eastertime.

*John Harrold*

## Calvary In Penarth

Here with the persuasive tide washing into land
I am motionless.
A man subdued by heaviness,
Lost in the passage of time.

Content?
Maybe a lamentable cry escapes me,
But, yes, I am content.

Yet inner turmoil dislodges my peace
I waver between good and bad days,
Hovering, lurching violently inside.

Why?
My answer is -
Why not?
A struggle cannot simply go away,
Its web of shiny stranded silk entangles my heart.

But as I smell the salty air
As I savour the fresh breeze and warm sunlight I sigh,
I cry one more drop of sorrow
And then move on.

My comfort is in Christ's cross
He bore it well
He bids me to bear mine now
I am never far from comfort at Calvary.

The sharp thorn crown pierces me
But I am strong in Him.
The pain passes because when I look again,
I am in paradise.

*Nigel Latham*

## *Faith Today*

There is so much talk of faith and belief
I wonder, what is it really all about.
Do we really pray to God and act like we do
Is that what made John the Baptist shout!

O generation of vipers, to whom did he refer?
Do those words apply to you and me.
I think they must, because there is very little proof
That today's world is different to when he

Met with Christ and the baptism took place
And God acknowledged Christ to be his son.
John then being prisoned, we all know his fate
But he knew, Christ's love he had won.

The words, as spoken by Jesus Christ
Man has chosen to twist or ignore
Over nineteen hundred years since Christ was killed
And it is said: It was for us, he died for.

He was put to death for the things that he said.
Man, for that sin, God his father could never forgive.
Is it too late? To heed and believe what Christ said
Turn the other cheek, love thy enemy, live and let live.

Some claim they represent God, here on earth,
And continuously refer to 'The Lord Jesus Christ' by name.
But do they honestly practice what Christ did preach
Or fear, like Jesus, they would be tried and crucified the same.

My faith is secure in the hands of Jesus Christ, I know
Only His way can make this world a fairer place for all,
Mankind must live the way Jesus said, as I believe that
God and Christ are as one, when you call.

*T W Denis Constance*

## *Easter Courage*

As heavenward swarms, my dearest wish
That all may realise they own
A piece, a swath, a garnished dish
Of England's claims, His feet did tread -
On these sweetly hills and valleys sown,
By His fair hand, that nails bore red.
In blood, He gave, that we may live, and see
Why you and I, must vergers be
Of sacred soil, so many died.
Transformed He rose, to heights sublime.

So here we stand, as fires burn
And must transcend, like butterflies
From this emotion, deep and sore
And build again, the land we bore.
From desolation, to glory fled,
In these our verdant hills,
Again to rise from ashes strewn.
Miracles, do so come to pass
With courage we'll survive, and soon
Determined, forward, may we surpass,
Our wildest dreams, the world to see,
That England stands, by its fair might
As fairies dance, and knights roam free
On this hallowed turf, that burning tree.

*Albert Boddison*

## *The Family Of Man*

There are only three sorts of people
In this world, men, women and children,
So isn't it about time we disregarded things
Like race colour or creed,
For it is only a matter of chance
Where any of us get born,
And to condemn anybody for the colour of
Their skin is utterly forlorn,
For don't they do the same as we do
When they lose a loved one, break down and cry?
Love and understanding is something that
Every one of us badly needs,
And in fact if we showed more of it to each
Other a far better world it would be indeed.
So let's stop being dogmatic and try to be
Understanding and kind,
And then in a very short time I am positive
That we will all find a far different attitude
Towards each other for after all really belong
To the very same clan,
And that is of course, 'The family of man'.

*A E Reynolds*

## *Spring Has Sprung!*

Little lambs so soft and clean
New upon the hill,
I feast my eyes and gently smile
Then linger on at will.
How dainty are their little jumps
How cute their little tails,
Ma, ma, ma they seem to cry
And beckon with their wails.
Their mothers come and gently nudge
The fluffy little mites,
'Don't stray too far' they seem to say
'And do not scale the heights.'
A perfect picture there they make
We all love them of course,
Especially on a Sunday noon
With lots of green mint sauce!

*Cheryl Mann*

## *Resurrection*

When flowers lift their little heads
Still blossoming within
When leaves begin to spread their wings
And early birds do sing
I feel a growing joy and hope
A lust for life and want
Awakened by a gentle breeze
Secret desires loom and bloom forthwith
I note the smile of interest
Below a handsome brow
I feel the sun's seductive warmth
Caress my helpless skin
My senses blur
I dream and dream and dream
'It's spring!'

*Karlena Jambor*

## *Untitled*

Look beyond death
to death's gift
and know that trees
and flowers lift
themselves beyond their
sad season
that we accept
without reason.
That is how things
are. We never
ask why and
so we sever
ourselves from
the unquaried gift
and in our silence
we never lift
ourselves beyond
ourselves. We die
long before we hear
death's cry.

*Jack Clancy*

## *From Death To Life*

On a hill long ago stood three crosses
The Holy Bible tells us so,
The middle cross my Lord was put to die
But he arose again for all - you know.

At Easter children love Easter eggs made of choc,
Some people love the sight of daffodils bright,
Many remember just how our Lord died
On that dark long, long, cold night.

The wind blew the Disciples fell fast asleep
As into that garden the soldiers all came,
They took away my Lord
And nailed him on the cross on the hill of shame.

At Easter now cach year I find a kind of joy
As I'm at ease - as of being set free,
For over and over I feel his closeness
For my Lord arose from death for me.

Then the cross on the hill goes from my mind
All the nails and the thorns that tore,
For at Eastertime each year
I kneel to thank him - that he arose for all.

He is now preparing a home for us
To be with him to live
So rejoice in our Lord
Come lost souls - 'Jesus still forgives'.

*Marion Staddon*

## *Easter*

To free us from sin He came to earth,
Was betrayed here by a friend;
That is such a bitter pill to take,
Though His life would never end.

He mixed with those unworthy,
He walked with those who care;
He prayed for those condemning Him,
The ones that failed to snare.

The cross is there but it is bare,
For Jesus Christ is risen;
The thorns the nails He bore for us,
So our sins are forgiven.

Not only on this special day,
Will you feel His love for you;
Knowing that it is meant to last,
All your lifetime through.

Rejoice now on this Easter Day,
With thanks for love and care;
Bring close lost souls who search to know,
Our Lord is always there.

   *Ivy Squires*

*Easter Communion*

And I beheld the glory of the Lord,
As I hastened to meet Him on Easter morn,
Running and slipping on the dewy grass
Until I reached Him standing on the lawn,
And put my hand in His; His steadying grace
Held firm my faltering feet: and all the world stood still:
And I think my heart was filled with glory too,
As I looked into His face.

*Daphne Foreman*

## *Easter*

The struggle, it is over.
Behind - the cross, the tomb.
Emerging from the darkness,
as from Thy mother's womb -
Alleluia, Jesus.
The victory is Thine.

The first to break the barrier.
The shrouds of death to tear.
Come through the clouds as sunshine.
The crown is Thine to wear.
Alleluia, Victor.
The Word - seen to be done.

Whoever soared to Paradise
without a taste of earth.
Its challenges to face them.
A war to wage from birth.
Alleluia, Saviour.
Now we may follow on.

*Daphne Robinson*

## *Easter*

Easter is a religious festival,
The perfume of the daffodils you can smell.
Time to make an Easter bonnet,
Your head, you'll wear upon it.
Time for the Easter bunnies and chicks to come out,
The children are excited, they scream and shout.
Their chocolate eggs, they cannot wait to eat as they come in all different sizes,
Some are short and small, while others are big and tall with sweets inside,
Don't forget to share them as there is nowhere to hide.

*Tina Rooney*

## *Easter*

I'd love to be 'Down Under' when
our Christmas time is here,
the summer sun and sparkling sea
of Bondi beach is near.
Eat turkey on the hottest day;
sing carols without snow:
keep Christmas in mid-summertime
with tales of long ago.

But soon comes autumn in the air,
the leaves begin to fall,
and Easter comes with lengthening nights -
it's wrap up time for all!
The flowering blooms sink back to earth
as nature says once more
'Ignore the Resurrection tale -
new life, new birth in store.'

It's oh to be in England now
that month of April's here
when all our vegetation buds
and warmer days draw near.
They speak of Resurrection as
they leap up, flowers unfold
to welcome 'Christ is risen today'
His glory to behold!

*Owen Edwards*

## *An Easter Egg Invasion*

An Easter egg invasion
That time's again at hand
In every supermarket
There in stacks, they stand

Gift-wrapped in fancy boxes
Death by chocolate it seems
Eggs to suit all ages
Filled with sweets, or sickly creams

White chocolate, dark chocolate
From giant size to small
There's no way you can escape them
In the supermarket hall

With all this Easter hype!
Many children will be spoiled
While others, just like me
On the day have their eggs boiled.

*Karl Jakobsen*

## *Easter*

On Easter Day God raised his son
who died at such a cost.
Soon life in Heaven had begun.
Christ won and Satan lost.

Sprays in church are beautiful
and such a cheerful sight.
All hymns and prayers are meaningful
and altar cloths so white.

The choir in their Sunday best
come through a polished door.
The priest makes sure that they are blessed
on such a spotless floor.

The sacred vessel's mystic light
and crucifix of gold
were polished and looked glowing bright
and shiny to behold.

A woman with a faithful few,
the cleaner of the church ill-shod,
offered from the furthest pew
her cleanliness to God.

*N Reeves*

## *Spirit Poem For Easter*

Tears fell like rain
The day he died
Heads bowed low in shame
Silent prayers whispered his name
The name of 'Jesus'.
O what a friend is he
Who came and died for us
That day at Calvary.
But death could not his silence hold
He rose and now the story's told
Forever more God's love we'll see
For through his death
We were set free.
All praise and glory to God above
With joyful hearts
We take, your love.

*Olga Johnson*

## *Spring Has Sprung!*

Trumpets of yellow upon my table
Sprouting from water within the vase.
Tightly closed buds of yesterday's picking
Still in their 'wrappers' encasing each flower.
All through the night they silently opened
Like fairies invisibly doing their work
Each petal revealing more yellow,
Each moment more splendour.
As dawn approaches
I rise from my bed
And enter the room,
What beauty!
Creation's work
At its best
Just for me,
Here
Now.

*Chrissie McGrew*

*Easter*

Easter is a festival of the resurrection of Christ.
With eggs and decorations; we celebrate so nice.
When Jesus came to life again; to spread the word, and give advice.
To people who did not believe; to give them faith in Christ.
To speak of love and happiness, instead of hate and war.
While people came from near and far; and listened; held in awe.
To think of how he rose again, from being nailed to that cross.
A man who came to life again, after such a loss.
So Easter is a time to give. To celebrate; have fun.
A time to believe in God, our Lord.
And in the resurrection of Jesus; his son.

*J R Dixon*

*Easter*

That cross, that a cross set high on a hill,
That cross, that cross, I can see Him still,
Rugged and stark like the darkening skies
With two others up there one on each side,
There He died!

He carried, He carried that cross made of wood,
Each step was torture, the stones were sharp.
But sharper, much shaper were the nails they drove in,
The pain was made worse by our treatment of Him,
There he died!

The sky, the sky was darkening now,
And Jesus cried out to His Father above,
He then died a cruel death for all people to see,
He'd taken our sins, paying the supreme penalty,
There He died!

But glory! Oh glory! He didn't stay there,
He rose from the grave and ascended on high,
Our debt was all paid, His blood set us free,
His Spirit was now given to guide you and me,
Father and Son are now reigning in heaven above,
He's alive, Hallelujah!

*Jean Smithers*

## *Good Friday*

I wish for skies so
blue and white with
sunshine warm this
Friday morn to celebrate
the Saviour's name
in our Easter Friday
march

In every town the
church folk meet
from Brownies to
brass bands
clean and neat
all the folk who came
to watch cheer the
procession as they
go by wearing bonnets
of Easter blue.

*Ernie Cummings*

## *We Do Not Listen*

We do not hear
what he has to say
as we have no wish to know.

Hidden in the folds
of what he has to say
is why we do not listen.
For what he says
makes hearing hard.

His death,
for he is now dead,
reveals the folds of his life
now speaks to our understanding.

We rejoice in our vision,
for what he has to say
is now clear.

We weep not at His death
but at His words
which now we hear:

'Death is the beginning
of your understanding'.

*Michael Alan Fenton*

## *Dominus Crucifixus*

Were you there when they crucified my Lord?
Deprived of water and starved of food:
The African child with his solemn sad eyes,
Too feeble to brush off a thousand flies,
His silence moves the aching heart
To give, in answer, in some small part
Ease for the suffering of his lifeless frame
And to pray for him, in the Saviour's name.

> Were you there when they crucified my Lord?
> In the lonely widow whose friends can't afford
> The time to visit, to sit, to talk
> Or even suggest a quiet walk -
> The active mind that cared for all
> Who, on her goodness chose to call -
> Neighbours, children, all who came
> Support her now - in the Saviour's name.

Were you there when they crucified my Lord?
Not for us to wield the sword
As Peter did at Gethsemane.
But to pray that the prisoner may be set free,
To work for freedom of others, to pray
To the Master for strength, along life's way
That nations may struggle afresh to claim
Peace for all, in the Saviour's name.

> Were you there when they crucified my Lord?
> When honesty and loyalty went by the board
> And, to save themselves, men lied and schemed
> Forgetting that sin made them not what they seemed,

When life was strange, and the soul cried out
In many a conflict and many a doubt,
Did you remember that God's Son surely came
That we might o'ercome, in the Saviour's name:

And by the cross and Passion may strive, and stay
To inherit the joy of Easter Day!

*M Keeling-Roberts*

## *Easter Sorrow, Easter Joy*

Joyful is as joyful does, in this we must believe,
For the advent of this Easter may flatter to deceive.
Portrayed there is stark contrast, to our Lord on the cross,
A world that fights within itself, and cannot see the loss.
It is for us to focus, as the Easter week begins,
To take a moment every day, remembering, for our sins,
How Jesus paid the price for us, and those who went before,
Lest we should fail to notice, when we slam God's open door.
So when you walk the stony road, towards the hilltop high,
Remember Christ on Calvary, and why he chose to die.
And when you walk through forest, dark and filled with gloom,
Give more than just a fleeting thought, to Jesus in the tomb.
And when you sin as we all do, in life's confusing day,
Consider Judas in that week, and the price our Saviour paid.
But as you think, remember, that from the cross He came,
Back to a world He loved so much, despite its human shame.
He vanished from Gethsemane, from mortal eyes and blame,
To rise again and show Himself, to those whose doubts remained.
So surely we can spare some time, to ponder on these things
During a week which long ago proclaimed the King of Kings.

*John Cook*

## Easter

'When do we celebrate Easter?' the teacher asked the class
She looked around and chose a child whose arm was waving fast.
'Easter starts on Boxing Day and lasts until September,'
The child replied with great aplomb, 'that's all that I remember.'
The teacher sighed and turned around to choose another student.
But all agreed the first was right, to disagree imprudent.

'Tell me the story of Jesus, who died upon the cross.'
The teacher glanced around the room, but everyone was lost.
A pupil who was struggling to tie his trainer laces
Said, 'Miss, we all eat chocolate eggs, it's time to stuff our faces.
You have to eat three hundred, and all in different ways,
It tells you on the adverts on the telly, every day.

The supermarkets fill the shelves with eggs on Boxing Day,
And you have until September to clear them all away.
For that's when Christmas time begins, and ends in late December,
And all the stores are full of toys, too many to remember.'
The teacher sighed and wondered how to teach her small consumers
That marketing successes were the reason for their bloomers.

'I'll tell you the story of Jesus, from a long time ago.'
'It's a story of love and compassion for friends and foe.
God sent his son to save the world, but he was crucified.
The Romans nailed him to a cross, and on that cross he died.
He died to save the sinners, he died for you and me.
He never heard of chocolate eggs, or supermarket tea!'

*Doreen Hanley*

## *Worship*

Why do you pay homage to the empty churches,
The silent choir-stalls and deserted pews,
The pious remnant of the faithful few
Clinging to ancient tradition and obsolete views?
'Why pay homage to the all this,' said my critical enquirer!

For the sake of the holy water
In the baptismal font,
By the token of the Cross,
In new life sanctified,
Is Christ born again.

For the agony of the Cross,
The private grief and pains
With Christ identified,
The cleansing and healing,
Blessing and absolution.

For the sake of the holy sacrifice,
The consecrated bread and wine
The words of the Priest softly intoned,
'This is my body,
This is my blood.'

The kneeling figures at the altar rail,
The invisible offering,
The church's body broken,
The living sacrifice,
All abide in Christ.

The solitary flame that burns over the altar,
Its watch maintains by day and night.
The light on the golden cross reflects
The victory over death.
*Christ is risen!*

*Beryl Johnson*

## *Eastertime*

Easter is almost here once again,
This time it is so sad because of pain,
Seeing so many cattle, sheep and lambs burnt,
Lessons never seem to be learnt!
Sun is shining on the countryside,
Little villages glow with local pride,
There are still many things to do and see,
Let's go and answer their urgent plea,
Enjoy a country walk on open track,
Visiting the local pub for meal or snack,
A happy day could still be had,
The villagers would then be so glad.

*Joan Miles*

## *The Death Of The Son*

I look to the place where the Master was slain
That old wooden cross where He carried my pain
And wondered why He had to suffer for me
Such a slow lonely death and indignity
I watch the blood flow from His hands and His side
That I may forever in heaven abide
And if I'd never done all the things that I've done
I would not have caused the death of the Son

For years I denied though the pain I could see
That the nails and the thorns had been put there for me
That the rivers of blood were my sins rolled away
As He closes His eyes at the end of the day
Of Father forgive them was His final cry
As He lay down His head and He started to die
I gaze up and look at the most perfect one
And I realise I've caused the death of the Son

They have taken Him down from that old wooden cross
And into a dark and damp tomb He was tossed
And a stone rolled across so nobody could see
The death of the Son in such indignity
But on the third day the tomb it was bare
The stone rolled away and nobody was there
And death is no more He has broken the chain
And for my redemption the Son liveth again

*David John Dunbar*

## Easter Glory

At Golgotha, that evening, all was still.
An empty cross in silhouette atop the hill.
The hubbub done, the watchers all gone home.
His body in the tomb behind the stone.

The Twelve in fear and doubt, their hope destroyed.
The promises He'd made - were they now void?
Were three years with Him really all for naught?
Where now the creed of love which He had taught?
Oh! All was gloom.

But hold - for suddenly it's Easter Day,
And see, the heavy stone's been rolled away.
The tomb is empty now - it was no prison -
And as He promised, so Our Lord is risen.

Now is the gloom of Friday all dispelled,
O'erthrown by faith and hope and love untold.
Let's shout aloud, with praise, this wondrous story -
The Son of God is risen in all His glory.

*Angus W MacDonald*

## *Easter*

Easter is when daffodils grow
and when animals are born.

Easter is in March or April
when the weather keeps changing.

Easter is when we get Easter eggs
and have the taste of chocolate
in our mouths all day.

Easter is only one day a year,
so enjoy it whilst it lasts.

*Dannika Webber*

## *The World Seems Now Too Crowded*

The world seems now too crowded
The trees are crowded out.
The green leaves seem susceptible
Each spring there seems a doubt
That they will reappear
When Easter's on its way.
The Lenten days are slow to move
We have to wait for May
But then are reassured
The country's safe once more.
It's Eastertime that does it
We see the open door.
The door that leads us onwards
To make us want to care
To cherish all we live for
And make us want to share
The good times and the hard times
The beginning and the end
And make us keep our friend.

*J S Games*

## *Easter Fun*

Yellow fluffy chickens
Laying golden eggs,
Funny how we swallow
All these silly things.

Easter is quite special
It brings the children joy,
To see the fluffy creatures
Wrapped in silver foil.

You must not open now
Your mother screams at you,
But round the other sofa,
You secretly - undo

Your fluffy little chicken
To see the golden egg
And now you start to swallow
The silver-covered - choccy egg.

*M Griffiths*

## *Lenten Blooming; Easter Glory*

Up out of the cold, dead winter ground
  appears a purple crocus
  delicate seemingly, unsure;
  yet blooming despite the cold air
  - sovereign of the equinox

Stiff in the spring breeze
  the sleeping dogwood's buds burst
  white surrounding blood-red fruit
  - cold death defied

Like hallelujah trumpets,
  the white lilies sound forth;
  azaleas,
    hydrangeas,
      wild roses,
        pansies,
          crab-apples,
            cherries
  all sing out!

  *John A Mills*

## Whoa! Darryl

When I was ten years old my mother took me to Willow Grove Mall
But not to play Donkey Kong or Pac-Man at all
I was taken to see the Easter Bunny
Something about my visit to him was very funny
When I walked over to him I sat on his lap
I told him that I wanted to act
In a movie called Oscar with Sylvester Stallone
He told me to leave show business alone
I'm the Easter Bunny not an entertainment lawyer
Find something different and more appropriate for you
I went home thinking about what he told me
The free advice the Easter Bunny sold me
About the movie business in nineteen forty-one
And how being an actor was far from fun
How much it was hard work in front of the public
Well then tell me exactly how Sylvester does it
So I took the advice of the Easter Bunny
And then told a job at Redner's Markets
Started making some good decent money
Forgot completely how acting started
When I was ten years old my mother took me to Willow Grove Mall
But not to play Donkey Kong or Pac-Man at all
I was taken to see the Easter Bunny
In a movie called Oscar with Sylvester Stallone
I'm the Easter Bunny not an entertainment lawyer
I went home thinking about what he told
So I took the advice from the Easter Bunny

*Harry Swanger*

## *Easter*

Easter, a time I sit in sombre silence,
Between the final hour of two and three,
And grieve for the son of God who died for me,
Ridicule and scorn, I suffer them too,
But I bear them all the better because of you,
You are in my heart and in my head,
Truly, the son of God is not dead,
We talk every day,
You are never too far away,
You are here beside me now in pewed company,
And always will be,
I will never be abandoned as we abandoned you,
On that lamented day,
Easter! Is everything to me because the son of God,
Died for me,
On that Friday at Calvary.

*Robert Henry Lonsdale*

## Judy Or Jesus It's Easter Again

A man on a cross;
Tiny tots with their telltales of contraband eggs,
A girl in a bonnet with ribbons of satin
And gingham and lace that showed off her legs.
With a voice that brought tears of sorrow and joy
And love for the first time to a girl and a boy.

But what of the man they nailed to the cross,
Were his efforts worth nothing
Now there's profit and loss.
Bishops as plump as church mice in the spring,
With limos and jewellery, without people to sing.

Churches that echo with voices of yore,
Churches for pigeons with locks on the door.
Ask the children,
Of Jesus to speak if they will,
'He plays soccer with style and lives in Brazil.'

*Doug Smith*

## Easter Day

We're gaithered in for Easter Day frae near at haund an far away
an ilka time, he has his say - The Resurrection.

Noo sit ye there an look aroond. What's set afore ye's been pit doon
by carin haunds wi love festooned - The Benefaction.

It's nae eneuch tae eat an gang. We need tae ken an 'gree amang
oorsels, the worldly thrang - an ither factors.

Sae syne afore ye tak the tea an cake, jist cast yer mind back
                                              for the sake
o' Him wha sits an does partake o what is offered.

We aa remember weel the day when Christ, oor Lord, was ta'en away
an' left for deid an on display, the Cross on high.

But noo we ken this glorious day we've naething lost.
He's here tae stay. Jist listen quiet an hear Him say
        The Resurrection, Life and Way!

*Andrew A Duncan*

## *Easter Memories*

Our Lord was crucified at Easter.
He died to save all our souls, on a cross that was heavy to bear.
Easter is also a time when young animals are born.
Fluffy chicks, baby lambs, leverets, or in other words baby hares.
Easter a time for Easter eggs,
And children looking for them everywhere.
Easter time means spring flowers.
Daffodils, tulips and hyacinths dancing in the breeze,
Pollyanthus with pretty flowers, really is a wheeze.

*Zoe French*

## *Easter's Almost Here*

At the end of winter, when everything seems dead,
Suddenly a change occurs - springtime's just ahead.
First arrive the snowdrops, crocuses as well,
Then primroses and celandines, deep down in the dell.
Next come golden daffodils, swaying in the breeze,
Birdsong in the garden, leaves and buds on trees.
In the fields the new-born lambs struggle to their feet,
Their mothers always close to them, eating grass so sweet.
All these things that happen at this special time of year,
Is nature's way of telling us that Easter's almost here.

*Margaret Whitton*

## *Easter Herald*
*(Dedicated to Beswick Church, Manchester)*

As Eastertide, it soon draws nigh,
Those chocolate eggs, we out to buy
Buttered buns are crossed and hot,
Good Friday message is not forgot.
In traffic queues to seaside town,
Remember he with thorny crown.
On stony hill had bore our strife,
For ransom paid eternal life.
We moan about the holiday rain,
Neglecting the one that carried pain.
Enjoy yourselves, though showers fall,
But have a thought, who died for all.
As clouds take flight from sunny ray,
A sign of life on Christ's third day.

*Andrew Bray*

*Easter*

Is sunshine showers
Soft morning dew
And early spring flowers
Life starting anew
Easter eggs
And Easter bonnets
With rabbits and daffodils
And ribbons upon it
A walk in the country
A trip by the sea
Life comes alive at
Easter for me

   *M Wise*

## Good Friday

Weep not for what they did to me
For I loved and forgave them all.
Rather these two commandments keep,
And listen when I call.

Love God - with all your heart, your mind,
Your soul and all your zeal.
Love one another - *as I have loved you* -
Then will my body heal.

   *Joyce Piper*

## *Easter*
### *Open up the window*
### *In the center of your chest*

Rumi said 'Open the window in the center of your chest
and allow spirits to fly in and out.'
It is within this magic kingdom that my imagination
awakens to the wonders of the mind.
Where have I gone that I do not find miracles?
What place within life's treasures
does not recognize the beauty of each morn?
If only I could teach you the beauty in a child's tear,
if only I could send you far beyond your midnight fears,
perhaps then you would know just why the sun does
choose to shine, the river seek its flow?
Open up the window and then seek your spirit's eye,
remember what the rainbow seeks beyond the starless sky.
It reaches towards the gates of God, in a wonder of its awe
and casts a shadow on the waters that doth clear life's waterfall.
What wonders doth the silence hold 'neath the flowers of your soul,
for the wisdom of the sage awaits when the half becomes a whole.
It is a miracle of splendour, wrapped in a cloak of light,
tied securely in forever 'neath a bow of endless flight.

*Kim Davenport*

## *Easter*

Here I stand before you a nervous quivering wreck
I only tried to sneak a look, may be pinch a little peck,
for the temptation now is so unreal I find it hard to fight
please, can't someone help me, get through this long dark night.

By using fluffy animals the add men hit their goal
and with just one more little step they'll take your very soul,
hooked, like a fish, now you are reeled in
and it's then that they convince you, addiction is not a sin.

And as yet another sweet wrapper, falls and hits the floor
you think of taking exercise, then stop and think what for,
it's as if you and your settee have just become as one
who said being a couch potato couldn't be good fun?

It's now, the dieticians come in . . . with such a heavy heart
for they know a chocoholic's diet will have to start,
and it's them that have to suffer the anguish and the pain
making someone real unhappy, but at least thin again.

So if there's anybody out there, and I know that you are
please I beg, be my hero, be my guiding star,
for I only need a little help to make it through the night
and a medium sized Easter egg should just about put that right.

*J R Hirst*

## *No Doubt*

I have no doubt,
That Christ is about,
The man from Galilee,
The one who died,
Was crucified upon the accursed tree.

He died in pain,
He took the blame upon the cross for me,
But now he's here,
He rose again and reigns in victory.

*Jean Thornton*

*Easter*

Through forty days and forty nights,
Our Lord was tempted, given frights;
He faced the tests before Him placed,
Not ever, once, was He disgraced.

He joined disciples, Upper Room,
They did not know what problems loom;
For Jesus knew that where they sat,
A traitor soon would on him spat.

He hung bedraggled, on the cross,
The world suffered tragic loss;
The body moved to sand based cave,
The stone in front, made it *His* grave.

Come Easter morn, the world in daze,
The Lord hath risen, folk were amazed;
The joy and shouts right o'er this earth,
Caused shocks as great as Christmas birth.

To risen Lord, we shout and praise,
Two thousand years, our glasses raise;
For those of us upon this land,
It's Easter greetings, play the band.

*John Paulley*

## Christ's Donkey

Where is the God gift
Sent to carry the sins of the world?
Where is the God gift?
The donkey demanded.
And then he snorted and then he brayed
And then he twitched his ears.

Can this be the God gift,
This tiny child?
Such narrow shoulders
To bear such a burden,
The donkey wondered.
And then he snorted and then he brayed
And then he stamped his feet.

This is the God gift
And I who brought his mother here
Shall take the babe away
When he bears man's burden,
The donkey vowed.
And then he snorted and then he brayed
And then he fell to his knees.

This is the God gift,
So why do you rejoice and sing hosannas
When you should weep for him?
The donkey asked.
And then he snorted and then he brayed
And then he blinked away a donkey's tears.

*Ted Harriott*

## *Easter Thoughts*

Rejoice, mankind, that on this Easter morn
        From death the Lord
Arose, that, conqu'ring death, might man re-born
        Believe the Word.

The very earth itself to life awakes
        From winter's grave,
And of the Son of God a symbol makes
        Who His Life gave.

For miracles of loveliness we see
        At Eastertide -
The soft spring flowers and green-budded tree
        It seemed had died.

Rejoice ye then, who by the Cross have griev'd,
        Bloom forth ye earth,
For from eternal death are ye repriev'd
        By God's rebirth.

    *Ruth Shallard*

## *Easter*

Easter; the day of Resurrection.
The day that Christ rose from the dead,
Victorious over Calvary
When for us He bled.

We rejoice now that He lives again,
Over are the solemn days of Lent
Over is the anguish felt by Mary
And over, the torture and the torment.

We, joyful in the knowledge that
He reigns, supreme above,
Hope to follow in His footsteps
From His teachings and His love.

With Easter, comes the thought of Spring,
Of young lambs and nesting birds,
Of daffodils and primroses,
And many sounds of Spring be heard.

Easter eggs for the children
And, no doubt, for parents too.
Easter greetings cards to send
And maybe some received by you.

Come Easter eve, people get busy
Our Parish Churches to adorn,
To make them bright and cheerful
To greet our Risen Lord.

*Judith Herrington*

## *The Samaritan Had The Essence*

Once paganism held all the world under its spell,
Now Christianity is an ancient faith as well.
Crucified and born again are the great issues stressed
When on new prospects the fervent Christian views are pressed.
Resurrection is the big point, but most of us find
It hardly matters compared to the need to be kind.
Centuries of theological effervescence,
Yet the Samaritan already had the essence.
Resurrection or not, it's the golden rule which could,
If practised by all, bring paradise to earth for good.

*Allan Bula*

## *Memory Of Easter*

Painted eggs on Good Friday morn
Hot cross buns from the baker - still warm
I remember it clearly - a little girl
In a pretty new frock and with long dark curls

I remember I could not understand -
If Jesus was dead, a really good man
And people sang hymns that were really sad
Why then, 'Good' Friday? It surely was bad?

On Saturday if the sun was bright
We would go to the park and sit by the lake
Mummy would pack a picnic to eat
And we were all warned not to wet our feet!

But Sunday was special in its own way
For Sunday really is Easter Day
Our church filled with daffodils - hymns full of gladness
Gone today the Good Friday sadness

Jesus, the vicar told us, had risen
A difficult thing to tell little children
I remember us little ones searching the sky
To see if He would be passing by

I remember my mother's pretty straw hat
And my father saying she looked good in that
And going to Granny's house for tea
And seeing our cousins and their new baby!

Easter for us was the real start of summer
With flowers abloom and the sun shining longer
But as we all know for children the best
Memory of Easter is eating the eggs!

*Norma Griffiths*

## The Long Journey (Friday 14th April 2000)

I looked through my window and did espy
A group of people passing by
With a banner held on high
And I wondered the reason why
On looking closer I could see
That they had with them a small donkey
I tried to think what it could be
Then it really dawned on me
They were walking the way of the cross
Throughout the parish right across
The donkey pilgrimage it was you see
Bearing witness for you and me
From Ripon Cathedral all the way
To Leeds on this momentous day
To lead up to the triumphant day
Of the other procession on Palm Sunday
What a very fitting start
Leading up to the very heart
Of the coming Easter Day
When, halleluia, we shall say

*Joyce Metcalfe*

## *A Special Time*

After the fasting days of Lent
There arrives a glittering event
Some having chosen to abstain
From cigs or booze, chocolate
      or swear words inane
Then arrives the Easter feast
All deprivations newly released.

They're boxed in every shape and size
Glittering wrapper, content surprise
Purple, green and silver bows
What's inside, nobody knows.

A shell of chocolate, dark, milk or white
Add to the sheer delight
'Mine has a chick on top'
'Mine's filled with marshmallow sloppy aflop'
'I've had two with one more to come'
'I feel sick, what's happened to my tum?'

Some have a gift as well in the box
Like a lovely selection of mouth-watering chocs
Some have a rabbit with big floppy ears
Whom you can cuddle and fill you with cheer.

This is in the celebration of the rising
      of the Lord
Who arose as our Saviour
We bear him in thought.

   *Gloria Hargreaves*

## *Eastertime*

Daffodils dancing
Spring lambs prancing
Bells ringing
Voices singing
Church doors open wide
Welcome, invites you inside
Easter is special to me
What does it mean to you?

*M Campbell*

## *When Easter Approaches*

The first days of Spring
Where buds on the trees
Are growing so daintily
Blossom and leaves
The daffodils dance on
The warm winds by day
New lambs are born
To the fields where they play
Easter approaches
The children delight
Waiting for Sunday
And wake early light
To them it's the treats
Of their chocolate and eggs
Excitement and laughter
All over the place
And then off to church
To remember this day
That Jesus had risen
To show us the way

*Jeanette Gaffney*

## *Rose And Apple*
### *(A Cappadocian Legend)*

'Dorotea, Dorotea,
Roses in thy lips I see,
Apples in thy cheeks of snow
- Whither goeth thou and these?'

'Teopilos, Teopilos,
Paradise is where I wend,
Where the apples never spoil,
Nor the roses lose their snow'

'Dorotea, Dorotea,
At the scaffold step I say
Roses red and apples white
- Send me these from Paradise!'

'Teopilos, Teopilos,
By the Blood that taketh me
Where the rose and apple fled
 - White and red I promise thee!'

Ere the rising tear had dried,
Ere the eyes had turned away,
Ere the head had turned to clay
All the heart had learned that day,

A child had come to proffer him,
Red with perfume and delight,
White for sweetness, cool as snow
- Rose and apple, winter-born.

'Theophilus, Theophilus,
Dorothea bids me say
She sendeth thee from Paradise
Roses white and apples red!'

Blood and snow were his that night!
- Theophilus, a Christian vowed,
Followed unto Paradise
Apples white and roses red!

*Beatrice Gwynn*

## *You Devil You*

Special time is Eastertime
To ignore the day is such a crime
I gaze upon those home-made eggs
Where chocolate shines in satin beds

Delicious dreams I have of you
In all your chocolate splendour
Dressed to kill, you have such skill
To make my heart surrender.

*Susan Olwen Papworth*

## *Egg-stacy*

Easter eggs
Don't have legs,
Unless they're from Chernobyl
But if they're from there
I wouldn't care
Them I would still gobble.

*Peter Miles*

## *Angel Watching*

As a boy I fell down
and a stranger helped me up . . .
There was a time when I was thirsty
and another lent a cup . . .

I know we should be kind
and show people that we care;
for angels pay us visits
even though we're unaware.

Every day I've lived
and faced whatever life would bring,
but I have yet to see a halo
or a single feathered wing.

My Father said, 'Seen or not
I'm sure they do all they can,
but an angel cannot change
whatever God has planned.

So stop looking for their wings
or a golden band above their head.
Don't look for flowing robes,
but upon their hands instead.

Son, you may never see them coming
nor hear them sing their psalms,
but remember He who helps us most
will have nail prints in His palms.'

*David E Nettles*

## Easter

What does Easter mean to me, as I look back through history,
The Bible tells of Jesus Christ, who did his best to save mankind.
To preach a gospel of love and compassion,
The struggle against cruelty and barbaric thoughts,
And as the Bible stories tell, he fed the hungry and healed the sick,
But a betrayal of trust meant his very end.
Crucified, nailed to a cross,
To all it seemed hope was lost,
And as he hung there with crown of thorns, he
Forgave all those who caused his pain,
And by the grace of God he would rise again.
And as the Bible story tells, that every year on Easter day
This resurrection will take place, and Jesus Christ will rise again.
But to all who celebrate with chocolate eggs and Easter cards,
Stop, reflect awhile.
If the Bible stories are true, what does Easter mean to you?
Is man's inhumanity really gone,
Did his sacrifice touch everyone?

*Thomas Usher*

## *Cancelled Debt*

Out of order, unable to pay;
No matter how hard we struggle,
We will never be in credit,
A downward spiral of debt on top of debt.

No hope, no way out,
Unless the debt can be written off.
But the account has to be zero for that to happen,
The overdraft still has to be paid.

So, what next?
Who's going to pay the overdraft?
The funding was made available 2000 years ago,
Enough to pay off everyone's debts.

There for the asking,
The debt can be refunded in full
And brought up to zero.
Debt written off, account closed.

*Kathy Rawstron*

## *Easter!*

A day for laughing
joking and having fun
eating the odd hot
cross bun.

Jesus Christ the
Lord who died
Christians all over
the world claim he
is magnified

Three days later
the great Lord
rose, he was the
Saviour his
heavenly father chose

Remember the
things thy Lord
has done he
gave his life for
you though yours
hadn't begun.

In heaven where
the streets paved
with gold the
protection of
your life is in
his heavenly hold.

*Cassy Dmore (14)*

## *An Easter Service*

Greetings and handshakes, friendly glances,
Arriving for a Good Friday service.
A burden of toil temporarily lifted,
As it's time to think and give thanks:

There is only a book to tell the story -
From diligent writers, two thousand years past;
He walked the Earth to teach and heal,
And without sin, was nailed to a cross.

Lead like a lamb to the slaughter;
His friends fled, to save their own skins.
Simon Peter heard a cock crow three times,
And wept as His punishment began.

A Roman spear pierced through His side,
As lots were cast for His garments.
In a pauper's grave He was laid for three days,
Then arose and breathed, to bring life.

*Phillip Stringer*

## *The Reality Of Easter*

At the cross I'm found when I fall.
At the cross You hear me call.
At the cross I give You my all -
Because You gave
Your all for me.

At the cross I find hope again.
At the cross You call my name.
At the cross I give You my pain -
Because You endured
The pain in my place.

*Natalie Jagger*

## *Easter*

A time for loving  
For sharing  
A time for not expecting  
Time to give thanks  
For all that we have been given  
And for what we take for granted  
A time for helping one another  
Of laughter and fun  
A time of being yourself  
And thanking God for His Son.

*Samantha Vaughan*

## I Wish That I Had Been There

I wish that I had been there
To feel your love first-hand
To kiss your feet and tenderly
Wash away the sand
I would have loved you Jesus
I love you so much now
The pain you bore to save my soul
With thorns upon your brow
My head is bowed in mortal shame -
The fear you must have felt
When they came to crucify you Lord
It was at your feet I knelt
Two thousand years have come and gone
And through all the changes wrought
Your love continues ever strong -
Shines through the battles fought
I hold your hand in fervent prayer
That all will live in light
And the sacrifice you made that day
Will guide us through this night

*Phillippa Benson*

## *Easter*

Mary saw the empty shell
Where there was once vitality.
She knew without a doubt
That this was no longer her 'Beloved'
He had moved on and left her.

Deep loneliness consumed her.
All her waking hours
She descended to the depths of despair
Wallowing in her misery.
Filling her whole being with negativity.

Exhausted, she finally slept
Dreaming that she was in a garden
Filled with the heady perfume of flowers
The joyful completion of bird songs
Illuminated by glorious sunlight.

After three days of rest Mary was gently wakened
Refreshed she went and told her friends of her vision.
Always know that Soul Love is forever,
It cannot die for the life of You
Resurrection takes place as soon as You allow it.

*Dolly Little*

## *Special Thoughts Of Easter*

Easter means so many contrasting things
So I will let my thoughts take wings
To me it is Calvary and the cross to ponder
A time for reflection and a time to wonder
Welcome to the springtime and pleasant sun
With hope of better days
When primroses pop their pretty heads from
The earth and byways
Children's competitions of egg rolling down
Some grassy green bower
Hot cross buns and lovely simnell cake so
Scrumptiously spicy to eat
So with all these things about Easter is so
Very hard to beat!

*Octavia Hornby*

## *Easter*

Why do the bells repeat
their mournful toll?
Death was not mere oblivion:
as one Man's death
has given Life to all.

Tears were shed for the Man.
Sorrow was felt for His flesh.
Now let joy rise for the Son
from our selfless souls:
His love blossoms afresh.

*Daniela Lampariello Taylor*

## *An Easter Verse*

Chocolate eggs and lots of treats
Lots of goodies for you to eat,
A little yellow chick
And beautiful daffodils for you to pick.

Eastertime is lots of fun -
Out walking in the springtime sun,
The little lambs they gently play
On this Easter holiday.

*E R Bridgewater*

## *The Precious Son*

The winter is now behind us.
    Snow, rain, and wind, have all gone away.
From the ground comes little green shoots,
    Spring, is on its way.

The snowdrops raise their tiny heads.
    How beautiful and white they are.
Nodding here, and nodding there,
    Bright and shining, like a star.

Crocus are the next to be seen,
    In colours of purple, yellow, and white.
Growing together amongst the grass.
    They are such a pretty sight.

Daffodils, with golden trumpets
    Look lovely, under the trees.
They tell us that Easter is almost here,
    As they dance about in the breeze.

Ash Wednesday follows Shrove Tuesday,
    This is the first day of Lent,
When for forty days, and forty nights
    In the wilderness, our Saviour went.

He was hungry, tired, and tempted.
    He had no shelter, and no home.
From the burning heat, to the cold of the night
    He had to wander, and roam.

Palm Sunday, He was loved by all.
    They cheered Him, as He rode along
On a little donkey, sure of foot
    Carrying his Master, who had done no wrong.

He knew that His life was about to end
        To save people, just like us.
In Holy Week, He was betrayed,
        Beaten, and hung on a cross.

That Good Friday, was a dark day
        As He suffered all alone.
He rose again, as it was foretold
        And showed Himself to everyone.

So, when we take our Communion,
        Just let us think what He has done.
How the Prince of Peace had to suffer,
        Although He was God's precious Son.

*Joan Smith*

## *Commercialism*

We sailed across to Israel
The holy land to see
We walked the path of Jesus
On his way to Calvary
Then to the church in Bethlehem
Where our Saviour he was born
In a manger laid with straw
One December morn.

I thought the prayers would roll off my lips
As I entered this holy place
Hands joined at the fingertips
Tears rolling down my face
Hurrying along the narrow streets
I came to realise
This holy place I had visited
Was too commercialised.

We walked on by the wailing - wall
Where the Jews they go to pray
The sun shone upon us
That warm April day
Then, there was a bomb alert
And away we were quickly led
I find I'm in a state more holy
When I say my prayers in bed.

*Sheila Graham*

## *Hosanna*

We look back remember the week before Jesus died,
When upon the cross, for us He was crucified.
How the crowds then extolled Him, shouting hosannas to a King,
Laying down their cloaks for Him waving palm branches they did sing.

He sent disciples for the donkey, which was walking with its mother,
A young colt unbroken, never ridden by another.
It stood still when Jesus mounted it, this to us foretold,
By Zeceriah the prophet, in the testament of old.

As He looked down on Jerusalem, Jesus did weep, and cry,
He knew what would happen in the future, the Jews that were to die.
He went into the temple, was upset, angry too,
At the money changing, the people there did do.

He upturned the many tables, of the wares upon the floor
As He expounded to them what the temple was really for.
A place for prayer, and worship to listen to God's word,
Then He healed the lame, sick, unseeing folk, all these miracles occurred.

Sometimes our lives are like the temple, wrong things have somehow crept in,
Maybe we need to take a look, throw away that sin.
Jesus still works many miracles, within our lives today,
His healing hands of mercy, taking our ills away.

Jesus is our King of peace, more precious than all the gold,
Worthy to be thanked, and praised, our ever gracious Lord.
Do we recognise this Jesus, extol Him as our King too,
Would you be ready, like the donkey, if tomorrow He came for you.

*E Griffin*

## *The Magic Of Easter*

In the earth, new life
Springing up there,
Majestic 'King Alfreds'
With bright yellow heads.
Like trumpets, blow in the wind
White snowdrops, mauve crocus,
And primrose so fair,
As if an artist has been there,
Sprinkling his colours on the ground.
Wee birds, the dawn chorus
Pair in nest, tree and grass,
Hunting for food, to take
To their young.

*Audrey Randall*

## *Eastertime*

When I think of Eastertime
I get all excited and think great
Easter eggs
My mum used to get me loads of
Easter eggs, so many Easter eggs
To choose from
Eggs, wonderful eggs
Chocolate delight, Eastertime
Friendly, wonderful, delightful time
Our Lord Jesus Christ rose
Give us thou thy eggs for Easter
Chocolate eggs, such lovely munchies
Given by a few
I enjoy upon Easter Day
These fine delights
Happy Easter
Eastertime
Weather outside sometimes sunny
Sometimes rainy
When rain I shall be in
Yes you've guessed
I'm munching on my wonderful chocolate eggs
Easter evening, a wonderful Easter meal
Then before bed
I can't go without another munch
Yes the chocolate egg
Oh Eastertime
I love
Now my boyfriend buys me Easter eggs
Plus I get my own
Yes yummy yummy
Eastertime

*Michelle Knight*

## Easter Bells

Ding, dong, ding,
Hear the church bells ring!
Ding, dong, ding, dong,
Sing an Easter song.
Ding, dong, ding, dong, ding,
Risen is the King.
Ding, dong, ding, dong, ding, dong,
Right will conquer wrong.

Ding, dong, ding,
Sunshine sparkling.
Ding, dong, ding, dong,
Raindrops splash along.
Ding, dong, ding, dong, ding,
All the flowers spring.
Ding, dong, ding, dong, ding, dong,
Summer won't be long.

*Gloria Joice*

*Easter*

Have you heard the wondrous story
Christ has risen up in glory -
He has burst forth from the tomb
Like a flower from its womb.

Holy women tell the story
Yes, they tell the story
Of Christ - of Christ in his glory
Alleluia, alleluia, alleluia.

The Apostles show surprise
But with them the story comes alive!
John outruns his brother
As they follow one another
Alleluia, alleluia, alleluia.

To the tomb they are bound -
For the Saviour must be found.
When they reach the open grave
An angel holds the stone
Alleluia, alleluia, alleluia.

Christ has risen up in glory
There is no end to this story -
Alleluia, alleluia, alleluia!

*Emily Hanney*

*Easter Is:-*

Chocolate, church, hot x buns
Love, friendships and moral sums,
Resurrection, forgiveness, re-birth and fresh start
- Christ's message at Easter to give us new heart.

*Betty Nevell*

## *Easter*

A day of rejoicing Easter is here
A time of hope, dispels all fear
A time to start life anew
To think of life with a different view
The message sent so loud and clear
There for all to see and hear
Sadly falling on many a deaf ear
What is this message sent so long ago
I have conquered pain and death
Risen from all agony and fear
To bring you hope of another life
One that is free from worry and strife
Rejoice again that Easter is here
With the promise of life evermore

*Kathleen Glover*

## *Easter Echoes*

A green island rises from sea-flooded plains.
Traders come from afar, bearing metals and strange objects.
A young man walks and talks -
People listen,
Puzzled and excited at the same time.

In the faraway place, years later,
The same man, older now, walks and talks -
People listen, then as earlier,
Puzzled and excited yet angry and challenging.
Light shines from his eyes
In the midst of the darkling, threatening world
That will not understand.

Then one Passover there is much noise,
And a meal in an upper room.
Whips crack, thorns draw blood,
Nails hammer through flesh and wood,
People cry out in anger and pain.
The light is put out, the darkness reigns.
Three days later the light leaps free.

On the green island friends somehow sense pain -
A pain they do not understand,
As they cannot explain why they hurt -
Only knowing that fate unfolds into tragedy.

Years later, a trader returns bearing stranger objects than before -
A simple wooden cup,
A thorn-bearing tree that blossoms so sweetly,
And news of a young man who died for our sins.

    *K E Warne*

## *What Easter Really Means*

Eastertime is here again
But what does it really mean?
Bunny rabbits, small yellow chicks,
Eggs wrapped in foil that gleam.

For me it means, so much more,
God's Son came to earth to die,
On a cross, He was nailed for us,
In a tomb His body would lie.

On the third day, at break of dawn,
The stone was rolled away,
Jesus had risen and was alive,
Death could not have its way.

Why did Jesus have to die?
Because of our sin and shame,
The gates of heaven would stay shut,
Outside we'd all remain.

Now the gates are opened wide
For all those, who will believe,
Jesus Christ lay down His life,
God's pardon we can receive.

God's mercy for the human race,
Was proven by love divine,
When Jesus the Saviour of the world,
Died for us at Eastertime.

    *Yvonne Charles*

## *Easter*

Eastertime is here once more,
The birds in the treetops call;
For on the cross at Calvary,
Jesus died to save us all.

The cattle in the meadow,
Graze in pastures lush and green;
Whilst lambs spring at their leisure,
So happy and serene.

Daffodils in the garden,
Are bursting into bloom;
Whilst church bells are appealing,
To bless the bride and groom.

Birds search in trees and hedgerows,
Making nests as they chirp and sing;
For nothing but the best will do,
To protect their young offspring.

Primroses along the bankside,
Show the beauty of nature's ability;
Whilst the ripples in the water,
Convey peace along with tranquillity.

Children tuck into chocolate eggs,
A tradition that goes back so far;
All of these gifts I appreciate,
When you think how lucky we are.

*Malcolm Goat*

## *The Judgement*

I saw a vision high in the archway -
Many superimposed faces peered down at me.
There in the church of Rydzyna, as the silver sheet raised,
God entered my heart and read my life,
Seeing my sins and private memories.

'Kneel before my Mother,' Christ commanded;
And glad I was to obey, for my knees
Weakened and gave way beneath me as my
Being filled with awe at the 'Presence'
Contained in the painting of Madonna and Child.

Sweet scent of incense curled its finger around me
As my sins were lifted away.
'Don't do it again,' God commanded, then was gone.
Dazed and bewildered I returned to my comrades
To gibber my story for days. But none understood
My ramblings. No words could convey the nakedness of
My sins before an unknown power.

*Marion Gray*

## *The Second Coming*
*(Beyond Resurrection)*

T he Time is now  
H e is risen and among us  
E ngaging others in the task  

S ending forth His apostles once more  
E nding centuries of searching,  
C oncealing nothing, loving all  
O nly giving, touching, healing,  
N ever ceasing; Great Spirit of hope  
D elivering always: Always delivering  

C hrist's Love to the Earth.  
O nly darkness shall fall while  
M an awaits a second deliverance.  
I t is upon us.  
N ow we shall see that  
G od has returned.  

I n Him this World is redeemed  
S aved from self-destruction.  

N o more betrayal, crucifixion and sacrifice  
O ne Easter is all eternity requires: But  
W ill you make His second time worthwhile?  

*Carole Wale*

## *Continuity*
*(Dedication: For Edith Mansfield, 1921-1977*
*Whose memory in our hearts is still written)*

Love is the magic of the age
As unwritten words
On a virgin page,
And lovers
Two unrehearsed players
On an empty stage.
Names and events are of no importance
For they neither capture or convey
Who or what you really are.
Know simply
That you are the love of the love
That which is part of and one with
The greater love.
Life is not a thousand paged novel
With a climax for an end;
It is the passing of loved ones
And the gaining of new friends.
Love is not a single moment
Or one treasured thought,
It is a continuous feeling
Striving with time never to be caught.
May the demise of life
Be short and free,
And may love continue to be.
Love is the magic of the age
As unwritten words
On a virgin page,
And lovers
Two unrehearsed players
On an empty stage.

    *Malcolm Peter Mansfield*

*Easter*

Easter was celebrated in our isles
In Saxon times, they say
There was a goddess of that name
And she had a special day

But well before that time, the Greeks
Knew the tale of Persephone fair
Who was wooed by Pluto to be his bride
And carried to his lair

And all the plants and animals
Were sad, they missed her so,
No young were born, no eggs were laid
And plants refused to grow

But Pluto saw his bride was sad
In Hades dark and drear
So he let the lady return to earth
For six months of the year

Then all things came to life again
The earth regained its breath
Birds laid their eggs, plants grew and bloomed
And life replaced grim death

So it's really not at all surprising
That Christians have good reason
To celebrate Christ's victory
In the ancient Easter season

For just as the plants and animals
Find a spring world to inherit
So we believe He conquered death
To live again in spirit.

*Elsie Karbacz*

## Easter Faith

When you think of Easter,
What comes to your mind?
A window full of chocolate eggs,
And cards of every kind.

> Daffodils and flowered moors,
> Fresh spring blowing breeze.
> The hiding sun has reappeared,
> To melt the winter freeze.

A time to spend with family,
And those you treasure dear.
Those who were distant reunite,
And hold each other near.

> Gifts of chocolate treats are given,
> And in return received.
> But selfishness has blinded us,
> And we remain deceived.

At Eastertime so long ago,
A person gave their life.
He died for other people's sins,
For poverty and strife.

> The true meaning of Easter,
> Should never be forgot.
> He gave his life and rose again,
> Forgiveness was his plot.

So next year when it's Easter,
Remember what's been said.
Faith lives on beyond all days,
And etches in your head.

*Sarah Bridges (13)*

## *Easter*

Jesus was celebrating Passover
When he said:
'My blood is this wine
My body is this bread.'

He went to pray
In a garden quiet
When a priest with guards
Came to Jesus with an attack.

On Good Friday
Jesus was hung on a cross
And was left to die
Jesus, dead was put in a cave.

On the first Easter Sunday
Mary came to see Jesus
But he was not there
The angels said he had risen.

Many times after
Jesus appeared to people
He didn't come for revenge
He came here to forgive.

*Lucy Adams (10)*

## *Easter Blessing*

Easter is the best
For undressing the eggs
For the quest of Christ
For sins to be forgiven
For blessings that he gave
For the enjoyment of kids
When they get their eggs
Easter eggs big or small,
It does not matter at all.

*Patricia Maloney*

*Easter*

Greet the Easter dawn
As hopes are reborn.
Son of God on Good Friday
Rises as spirit on Sunday.
People are aware
Of a listener
To their prayer.
Spring on earth waits until
The star-like daffodil
Waves a leafy frond
Like a magic wand.
In March breezes
Euphoria pleases.
Coins in a wishing well,
Think prayer or spell.
Wedding bells chime
To herald a time
Of new life
For husband and wife.
Along life's way
In trials of day
Dark hours followed by light
Cares take flight
April's sun and showers from Heaven above
Bring powers blessed with love.

*Sylvia Berwick*

*Eastertime*

Eggs, chickens, bunnies, candles,
Bonnets, daffodils, new sandals,
Blue and yellow - sunny skies,
Church bells ringing, birds on high,
Christ is risen, the world's renewed,
Time to shake off winter's mood,
Feel the hope now Easter's here,
With spring the glorious time of year.

*Marie Knowles*

## *Easter Matters!*

God came from heaven into His world
- He chose to, He didn't have to.
He lived perfectly.
He died in our place.
He was made sin for us.

People took Him,
Tortured Him by flogging,
   putting nails through His hands, His feet,
   putting Him on His cross to die
He chose to stay there - He didn't have to.

God, His Father turned away.
He couldn't look on sin, His Son made sin for us.
The Lord Jesus Christ, the Son of God cried out,
   'My God, my God, why have you forsaken Me?'
He died.

Men made sure of His death,
   piercing His side,
Death couldn't hold Him.
God the Father turned back,
   empty cross, empty tomb.
He raised God the Son to life,
   everlasting, permanent, eternal, perfect life.
It was all for you and me.

   *Rosalind Weaver*

## *Easter Day*

Seeing 'Meet me in St Louis'.
The sweet smell of daffodils. Glowing yellow
ducks, cracking foil wrapped chocolate
and carved bunnies. Palm leaf crosses
and burnt incense. Eggs that were painted
strange colours like cochineal, eggshell yellow
that looked anything but the colour of eggshells.
Getting mugs with my name on them and being
read every story ever written about ducks and rabbits.
Not having to wait any longer to get Cadbury's cream eggs.
Making cards and hats for competitions.
Having to watch the 10 Commandments
and trying to see if there are really 10 things written on those stones.
Vanilla candles, making cakes and chocolate nests
but wanting to make mine into hedgehogs.
Going to my grandma's who smelt of
lavender and tea, having dinner with tinned
potatoes and chunky mint I chopped from her garden.
The inevitably bad weather with it being a holiday.
Getting new cotton pyjamas to wear on Easter eve.

*Linda M Adams*

## *Easter*

Easter has always been a special time for me
In days gone by church in the morning then onto Grandma's for tea
When we were quite young we carried our Easter eggs for her to see.
I remember too, sometimes the walk was long in weather
Quite cold, great icicles from snowy roofs did hang.
Glittering like stars in the bright winter sunshine.

As I grew older, the true meaning of Easter was made clear
Our Lord was crucified and then risen, unseen for a while from
those who held him dear.
I was taught by the Sisters of St Peter's Community of Kilburn,
During the days of The Battle of Britain while London did burn,
They taught us that like our Lord we would rise again,
In peace, love, and laughter we could rejoice again.

Easter Saturday nineteen thousand and forty-six,
Doug and I were married in his village church.
Friends and family gathered in the flower bedecked church,
Blessed are they the sun shines on.

Easter Saturday two thousand and one, six children born,
Doug and I still together, fifty-five years on.
A new wedding ring replaces the old one, quite worn through.
Easter a time of holiness, happiness and learning still
The bells of our churches, telling of the old story 2000 years on.

*Kathleen Collins*

## *Easter Mass*

The sustained treble of the organ
Quivers expectantly in the tense air,
A hush, a sweet angelic stillness
Breathes on the crowd waiting to adore
The Lord of Hosts in all His glory.
Then suddenly - a thousand angels
Crowding about the altar wait for Him -
A vast and hidden choir sings praises
Filling the sanctuary with their hymn -
'O Ecce Panis Angelorum!'
The organ trembles into silence,
Softly a bell warms all - the time has come!
The sacred bread is raised on high -
Death has been conquered - see the Lord is here
Triumphant in His Resurrection!

*John Paget*

*Easter*

Subtle smells are
wafted o'er the universe
where drift
rose and cinnamon
lavender and thyme

These the noble poet greets
sketching in verse
sweet-scented memories
in a pleasing rhyme

A fragrant smell
releases energies -
      gentle
      vital
      pure

Felt like a charm
its roving stealth filters
through aromatic trees
      where
      nature's
      sweet song

The bird-poet
      sings

*Angus Richmond*

## *The Beauty Of Easter*

When Jesus carried His cross to Calvary
He knew, He had to suffer, to set us free
Free from our sins, when He died on the cross
As He shed His blood, and paid the cost

When Jesus triumphantly arose on the third day
He left His Spirit behind, to teach us to pray
Pray that we should not be led to temptation
To know that we have come to His salvation

When Jesus died, and arose for all mankind
That we should be forgiven, in soul and mind
When we go through life, with trials and tribulations
God will be there, to see us through, with His beautification

God has said, He will never forsake us, the truest word
When we trust, and believe in Jesus, our Saviour and Lord
Our God that keeps us, when troubles are nigh
And looks down upon us, from Heaven high

So when Easter is here once again
We should count our blessings and then regain
The richness of the risen Lord Jesus, who rose from the grave
Who gave us life, and the wonders He gave

God loves each one, whichever way we turn
But He wants each one, to come to Him, and learn
The wisdom the wonders, the miracles, which He did perform
When we turn away from our sins, and simply reform

*Jean P Edwards McGovern*

## *Eggs*

Have you some special memories
  of eggs on Easter Day?
Cream-filled? Nougat? Milk choc? Plain?
  Excesses all the way?

This year I'm in Franconia:
  a pleasant, warming sun
and folk of more inventive mind -
  relaxing, friendly fun.

For every well and fountain here
  with coloured eggs is decked;
each egg with brilliant patterns splashed,
  or subtle tints is flecked.

And should there be no fountain, then
  a water tub will do
adorned with flowers and Easter hares
  and eggs of every hue.

At home, more coloured hard-boiled eggs
  await us in a bowl.
At breakfast time we clash them:
  hers cracks and *mine* stays whole.

Such art-full, artless pleasures are
  too simple for your taste?
You'd rather gorge on cocoa-bean
  and never mind the waist?
  And never mind the waste.

  *Harold Wonham*

## *Easter*

Easter brings us gladness,
All the flowers are springing forth,
Every bud is bursting,
And birds singing all their worth.

Little chicks appearing out of
Their egg prison shell,
All this new life surely
Rings for us a bell.

It tells us of a Saviour,
Who rose up from the dead,
And reminds us too, that He
For us His blood has shed.

He died to make this possible
That we should His glory share,
That we might go to heaven,
And be with Him there.

*Nan Downs*

## *Rebirth*

It's spring! It's spring! The children sing
what will our Easter bunny bring?
Easter eggs of chocolate sweet
we look forward to this special treat.
Sunny days that warm the air
and Easter bonnets for us to wear.
Daffodils on tall green stems
and violets set like sapphire gems.
Catkins hang from trees so tall
and yellow chicks so soft and small,
cuddly lambs they leap and bound
and baby rabbits that make no sound
leave their burrows to greet the world
with fluffy tails all white and curled.
And long ago in suffering pain
Jesus died and rose again
so we shall all forever live
it's such a wondrous gift to give
just like all things upon the Earth
they're born again, a new rebirth.

*Neata Todd*

*Eastertime*

Frisky bunnies, Easter eggs
New-born lambs on shaky legs
Tiny chicks chip their shells
Churches ring their cheerful bells
To us the message they convey
Calling us to sing and pray
On that green hill far away
We know what happened on that day
Our dear Lord hung in awesome pain
So that we might live again.

*Doris Lilian Critchley*

## *Teuton Queen*

The Teuton Queen glides through the air,
   Golden daffodils watch and stare,
Her resurrection has come at last,
   Old winter is long gone and past.

She's the goddess of nature's earth,
   Rejoice and praise in greatest mirth,
Birds arouse, they sweetly sing,
   Bringing in the brand new spring.

Beautiful blossom fill the trees,
   Perfumed by a warm gentle breeze,
April showers clear the skies,
   A new-born baby softly cries.

Mad March hares box and run,
   Dandelions dance and have their fun,
Children pucker from all around,
   Sugar eggs they have found.

Brooks that gurgle through the wood,
   Where the snowdrops daintily stood,
Lambs bleat on in meadows green,
   She is here, our Teuton Queen.

    *Andrew Perrins*

## A Paschal Sun

A paschal sun awakes unseen, as misting fronds are stirred,
from untimely lazing, on the green.
Good wintered corbies, each one a thief, gather mooting, for
dew peeping molluscs, hard beneath.
Saffron trumpets outbrazen early light, disputing brilliance in
a bulbous commonwealth.
Which triumphs dark and grey pink streak, till slow at first, the
stippled orange and magenta speak.
Proud vanguard of the nearing light, whose crown, is daily raised,
till dark and danger is affright.
To promise life that sinning bore, that glory lies in vigil's watch,
on loving's ever, constant shore.
For night has but a robber's sway, that blustered fear does task,
and loses, yet to risen day.
Fast now the paschal sun grows hale and leads a promise by the
palm,
renewing vows, that melt travail.
For stone can keep no promise slave, nor mausoleum hold a soul,
against, a brightly barren cave.
At last, the paschal sun now full in power, exiles bones to unfetter,
life, to hear this sinless hour.
For nightness cedes its mastered fear, and joy's dominion, sways
those who feel, resurgent tear.
That liberating brine filled splash, that won for life a limitless span,
across a thorny, scourging lash.
That Easter dawn, now Paschal Son, the lamb that bore no sin,
completing morn, as life begun.

*Francis McDermott*

## *Easter*

That gracious humble man
Who died upon a cross
Did not think it strange that
Leaving heaven was a loss
He came to walk amongst those
Not thought much about
The weak, the frail, the sick
To give them hope to sing and shout
Because He rose again on Easter Day
Not only then but now
He is everything to those who walk His way
He's my Saviour He gave His life for me
When He died that so long ago day
Now I'm saved for all eternity
If my sins I confess and repent
He's everything to me, my hope and joy
This Saviour who from heaven was sent
This humble gracious man
Who died upon a cross
Giving His life that we might live
Was certainly no loss

*K Baird*

## *Remember This*

Easter is a time for remembering,
To give thanks to the one who made it possible,
He gave his life to save us all,
Even yet, his virtues we must extol,

Lest we forget what he gave up,
No man could ever know his pain,
Do not forget what he endured!
The effect of those sticks and stones will long remain.

This life he gave up for all mankind,
The miracle of resurrection from the grave,
Still astonishes believers
At his great courage show, for us to save.

In modern times the exchange of eggs at Easter,
Strangely, brings back memories of Jesus,
Eggs can be chocolate, or so hard boiled
That caricatures can be painted thus.

Children take care to be individual,
The joy is in the doing, before the picnic,
When with sandwiches and milk
They take to the hills, where on getting to the top

They have an egg rolling contest,
To see which egg can go furthest
Before getting cracked,
The fresh air affects the system.

So shortly they tuck into their hard eggs,
With much jollity and glee,
They are making the best of their life,
And praising the Lord for enduring strife.

*Mary Lawson*

## Simon's Story

The Roman soldiers seized me and I feared their intent
Searching in my head for any errors I had made.
Then they pointed me towards the rough beam of a cross.
Terror filled my mind - 'This surely could not be?'
'Carry that and follow behind him,' they harshly snapped.
I noticed then the man who was surrounded by the guards,
Staggering bruised and blood-stained along the stony path.
The crowds were gathered, jostling, jeering at the sight,
Flies buzzing round his wounds, mean and compassionless.
And what was that I saw, pressed hard upon his brow?
It seemed to be a crown - yes, a cruel crown of thorns.
I stood transfixed and stared, then because I had no choice
Of this macabre procession I too became a part.
His wounds from awful beating were clear before my eyes
As he slowly struggled forwards up that track of pain.
I did not know for what he was condemned to die this way,
But in his manner there was such a deep and strange calm.
Not resignation, but a brave acceptance and a peace.
I questioned in myself, with wonder, how this could be so -
That he who was to die, in such a way, and treated thus,
Was quiet and calm, yielded - whilst those who were to live,
In agitation, malice, scorn and bitterness cried out.
Who was this man who silently before them showed such peace?
Challenged that at first, I had thought only of myself -
The fear of being ridiculed and made to walk this path -
I now in some odd way felt privileged to be
Identified with this courageous man I did not know.
At last freed from the task, I found I could not then move on.
I stayed and heard the words that he spoke whilst crucified.
Forgiveness - when surely he should have vengeance sought?
I saw and wept at the great agony he suffered there.
The earth was chilled and darkened as if sharing in his pain.
And finally I saw his broken body taken down
And I continued, grieving, to reach my journey's end.
But later the news came - that he had risen from the dead.

What excitement filled my soul, for I now surely know
That gracious man of sorrows is truly God's own son
And I have been identified with him, what privilege!
My life can never be the same since God has intervened.
Forgiven! I will gladly share with others this great news:
*Yes, Jesus who is Christ the Lord*
*Is risen from the dead!*

*Jennie Metcalfe*

## *Easter Message*

Dark earth is stirring, awake and alert,
Easter approaches - symbol of rebirth.
Trees wear new leaves; flowers bend in the breeze,
Birds swoop, thieving twigs for the nests they weave.

In Britain's valleys there is great unease,
Thundering silence as mute farmers grieve.
Dreaded 'foot and mouth' has gripped our nation
We watch herds being culled in strict rotation.

Saturation cover the horror tales we're fed
Till brain washed, we believe all herds are dead.
Stunned, we tremble, a people in mourning
While tourism crumbles under the warning.

Oh we of little faith - think of tomorrow,
Let's curb our excess of grief and sorrow.
Next Easter we'll witness our salvation
And give thanks to God for his creation.

*Kathleen Potter*

*Easter*

Easter means so much to me
as much as each and every day.
A celebration party with an
enormous chocolate cake.
After I blow the candles out
I always make a wish.
Then I take a slice of cake
and put it on a dish.

*Valerie Gaynor*

*Easter*

My friend Molly says
the Easter bunny is seven feet tall
and it's pink
and it's magical
it visits all the children of the world
and it lays chocolate eggs
and no one ever sees it.

Since it's Easter, Mom says adults are allowed to
start drinking wine at breakfast time.
Mom says we have to find the eggs
before the birds do,
then we take the eggs up the hill behind the house
and throw them off, for the birds.

This is because Jesus died on the cross.
Which I think is sad,
he was only born three months ago at Christmas.
The Romans killed him
because he had a donkey named Judas.
Then Jesus came back to life
and escaped from his chocolate tomb.

My magic chocolate egg has the word 'Snickers' written on it.
Molly got a chocolate rabbit in a box with a Barbie doll
but her mom said it was still an egg.

If I could change Easter,
I would still have eggs but they would be solid chocolate.
When I pray to Jesus, he would answer me.
Dad would come and look for eggs with us
instead of watching the sport
and we would all eat lunch together.

*Jason Donald*

## Easter

Easter is the time of year,
When Easter eggs appear,
Full of joy and lots of cheer.

Now it's spring,
The church bells ring
To celebrate our King (Jesus).

*Abbie Latham (9)*

## *The Blessings Of Eastertide*

To count the blessings of Eastertide
Gaze around at the rolling countryside,
See the golden daffodils waving in
The gentle breeze
Stirring the new green leaves
Upon the trees,
Hearts ease violets and pansies
Peep above the ground
Far from the slippy mossy ground.

This new life upon mother earth
Reminds us all of the new birth
Which comes with every early spring
A message from God it does bring
Staring with the Crucifixion,
Then there comes the Resurrection,
Promising each man, woman
And child every happiness,
In the blessings of God's great
Love for us
Which are with us now and evermore
Surrounded by the spring flowers
Scattered on the earthly floor.

*Blanche Rice*

## *Sing For Easter*

Sing for Easter!
It's Easter, Jesus rose alive,
Defeated evil and its strive,
By His cross made humankind save,
Liberated it from sins,
Easter is victory for the Christians!
They got salvation from Jesus,
So committed to love Jesus!
It's Easter the love of Jesus,
The great love ever,
Never cost as high as Jesus' life, ever!
His great life sacrifice for us,
He gave the supreme divine love to us,
So great and wonderful Easter!
It's Jesus' great victory, Easter,
The ever living Jesus' Easter,
The everlasting Jesus' love of Easter!
Sing for Jesus in Easter.

*Jalil Kasto*

*Eastertide*

Easter, time of celebration,
end of fasting, time of feasting
lovers' meetings, reconciling,
no more school for precious weeks
journeys home from distant places
gatherings for the Easter service,
joyful hearts or quiet endurance,

crowded congregations, families
friends relations too, all ages,
while the Easter candle is lit,
symbol of the Resurrection;
waiting for the start of service,
people raise their hearts and voices
invite God in, take Communion,

pray for peace, make new choices
enjoy the flowers and the music,
thankfully relax, reflection, and
the mood for new beginnings,
thankfulness that Lent is over,
and, for a short hour, peace reigns.

*Monica Redhead*

## *Silence This Easter*

The silent spring
Struck still
Still air no sound
So shocked I feel numb
This silence is not through peace and tranquillity

The fields lack movement
Without the reproduction of new-born
Calves lambs and piglets
The continuation of life is lost

My children ask 'Where are all the baby lambs?'
It is difficult for me to explain
When they are older they will ascertain
This slaughter so shocking
Ceasement of life to innocent animals
This tragic holocaust

I tell my children the lambs are
Having a longer sleep this year
Because the weather is colder
They will know more when they are older

*M Wood*

## *Easter Hope*

Hope is like a whisper
Borne upon the breeze,
Like the nectar from a rosebud
Carried by the bees,
It fills the heart with fragrance
Spills out upon the air
An illuminating radiance
Where there was once despair.

Hope is God's quiet message
That steals into our heart
When we have lost a loved one
And former things depart,
It will not be defeated
It's real as you and I,
Serenity its object,
No doubting can belie.

Hope was born at Easter,
God knowing we are frail
Shows in convincing fashion
That His promise cannot fail,
And as all Nature's wonders
Are resurrected upon earth,
My grateful heart still ponders
What His sacrifice was worth!

*O Miller*

*Easter Deer*

Easter Sunday, what will you do?
I shall sit in my garden, enjoying the view,
Blossom on the trees, rhubarb shooting leaves,
Garden taking shape, as we enjoy the Easter break.

Squirrels running high and low,
Jumping from branch to branch, off they go,
The smell of freshly cut grass,
The seedlings planted, growing at last.

Easter means a lot of things to me,
The start of spring most importantly,
With all that grows in my garden near,
I can sit and imagine, free running deer.

*Joanna Dicks*